Journeys to Orthodoxy

A Collection of Essays by Converts
to Orthodox Christianity

edited, and with an Introduction by

Thomas Doulis

"In Him was life and the life was the light of men" (John 1:4).

Light and Life Publishing Company
Minneapolis, Minnesota
1986

Light and Life Publishing Company
P.O. Box 26421
Minneapolis, Minnesota 55426-0421

ISBN 0-937032-42-5

The icon of the Pantocrator on the cover is the work of David Giffey and is in the dome of Assumption Greek Orthodox Church, Madison, Wisconsin.

TABLE OF CONTENTS

"Preface"

The idea for this book developed during the moments before a Luncheon at the 27th Clergy-Laity Congress of the Greek Orthodox Archdiocese.

The convert-delegates from various communities throughout the Archdiocese were a reminder that the women and men who had espoused Orthodox Christianity in America represented a never fully assessed or understood force in our Greek Orthodox communities. But it was the soft-spoken, bearded iconographer who led me to ask why he had entered the Orthodox Church. Because we had to find the tables where our delegations sat, we had little time to talk. What I managed to hear before we went our separate ways, however, was intriguing and enigmatic.

Someone should do a book on converts to Orthodox Christianity, I said when I found my table. Converts were gradually taking their places in the intellectual and spiritual leadership of Orthodoxy in the New World, but most birthright Orthodox either continued to think of their Church as an ethnic preserve not to be scrutinized or taken seriously, or were discovering how complex and rich their intellectual tradition was and unable to devote time to assessing the present condition of their Faith.

Was such a book possible? The priest who asked the question was unfamiliar to me. To this day I don't know why Father Anthony Coniaris was sitting among our delegation at the table. I thought so, I replied, suddenly not sure of myself. If and when the book ever came to be written, he said, ''Light and Life'' would be willing to publish it.

The essays did not exist. It would not be like anthologizing work already published and asking the writers to revise for a specific readership. Who would write the essays? I had spoken to only one person, but he did not have an essay written. How would the others be found? And when and if I found them, how could I be sure the contributors could write? And supposing they could write, how could I be sure their stories would be interesting? Besides, I had literary projects to last me a decade. In fact, I should not have been in New York in the first place. I had gone

5

to the Clergy-Laity Congress because an emergency had compelled the president of the parish council to cancel his plans to represent Holy Trinity of Portland, Oregon. I was just an alternate. It was a busy time for me.

I returned home, upset at myself for getting involved in such an open-ended challenge. But I wrote letters to fifty sources, requesting the names and addresses of possible contributors, hoping the essays would represent as many jurisdictions and conversion experiences as possible. I whittled the initial list down to manageable proportions, going from an unwieldly thirty, to nineteen, to the present ten.

During the year that these essays were in preparation, no writer was aware of what the others were writing; in fact, it was not until the middle of June 1985 that I was able to send out a partial list of contributors' names. The present essays, therefore, have been written independently, without the contributors knowing that they agreed or disagreed with others. Though asked to consider certain issues, each had personal concerns and reasons for conversion. My role, as I saw it, was to see where their interests led them and to make sure they did justice to their preoccupations. They had full freedom of expression, even to the point where I tolerated certain stylistic quirks and inconsistencies.

Finally, I would like to thank Mrs. Elizabeth Franklin of the Holy Trinity parish in Portland, Oregon for the many hours of typing she volunteered. Without her help, I doubt that *Journeys to Orthodoxy* would have been completed on schedule.

Introduction

Orthodox Christianity, though its adherents now number well over six million in the United States, is the great unknown among American religious denominations. Up to the past decade, it had been an almost exclusively ethnic branch of American Christianity, and since few of our countrymen exhibit an interest in the history or doctrinal content of Christianity, Orthodoxy has tended to be obscured by the more innovative and declamatory sects. Because it has until recently been a virtually tribal domain, the converts it has attracted were largely spouses who accepted its quaintness because of the richness and variety of its cultural resources. For their birthright partners, of course, the religion summed up the ethnic identity into which they had been born. The converts, however, since they began to take a clear and informed interest in the religion their husbands or wives assumed they knew merely because they had been born into it, more frequently got the better of the bargain. The witness of the converts by marriage is certainly an important one, but this book is about another kind of conversion experience.

The essays in *Journeys to Orthodoxy* are by and large products of the intellectual climate of the 1960s and 1970s. Vietnam, the drug culture, Vatican II, the liturgical innovations and ordination of women in the Episcopal Church, Yoga and Eastern (Asian) mysticism, the Jesus Movement, and Campus Crusade for Christ are all mentioned as key elements in the attitudes and culture from which the contributors emerged. One of the "side-effects of the Vietnam ordeal was the questioning of all authority," is how Father Tom Avramis puts it. The spiritual turmoil and intellectual upheaval created an environment where the most basic assumption of Americans, and Westerners in general, were challenged. The Evangelical movement, a reaction to much of this, occurred concurrently with the social and political agitation, but for some contributors its assumptions merely provided a springboard to the discovery of the Orthodox tradition and its profundity.

7

Almost all contributors dispute the conventional impression that — because of Saint Paul's experience on the road to Damascus — is considered characteristic of conversion: a sudden, blinding, and emotional conviction. In fact, the present testimonies document the slow, gradual development that led to Orthodox Christianity.

As many contributors found their way into the "Church of the New Testament" by chance or coincidence as by concerted study. Some attended liturgy, some, like Susan McShane and Father Anthony Scott, were introduced by relatives who had found their way before them, others like Victoria Smith and Maria King had reached impasses of one sort or another in their lives. Aside from the immediate apprehension of awe and beauty, the path to conversion for the contributors was in many cases unhurried, perhaps reluctant. Some were immediately accepted with love as part of the Orthodox communities, others found obstacles in their way, fears that their wishes to affiliate were shallow. "The Orthodox Church is not something you go through," Maria King was warned by the defensive priest. "It is for life." David Giffey, who went on to become an iconographer, found himself unwilling to jettison the religious insights and experiences that had led him to the Church. In fact, his witness is a moving account of the richness and variety, when informed by love and patristic knowledge, that converts can bring to Orthodox communities.

All contributors stress the fact that conversion is an ongoing experience and reject vigorously the assumption that there is nothing else after "initial commitment" to Christ. "I grew to realize that as important as acceptance of Christ may be," Father John Morris says "this is only the beginning of Christian life."

For all converts, Orthodoxy acted as a liberating experience. Fathers Anthony Scott, Paul O'Callaghan, and John Morris found that the teachings and Tradition of the Orthodox Church were a liberation from the legalism, the rationalism, and the guilt built into the system of Western Christianity. For Father Anthony, Orthodoxy entered his life as a "thief in the night", offering a "glorious sacred materialism without the guilt" his Baptist background had led him to believe was endemic to Christianity. Father Paul found Orthodoxy an avenue away from the sterile Protestant-Roman Catholic dilemma, which was a legacy of Western Christianity, where the "innovations of Rome and the reactions of the Protestant churches" had crystallized into positions that were not reviewed. And nowadays, Protestantism seemed to offer little but the "stark alternatives of Fundamentalism and Liberalism." Father John, trained as a historian before going on to study for the priesthood, saw that the great division in Christianity was "not between Catholicism and Protestantism but between Eastern and Western thought", since Westerners, knowing little of the mysticism of the Eastern Church, "follow(ed) patterns of thought stemming from Augustine as distilled by Medieval scholasticism and post-Renaissance" theology.

The reasons for the attractiveness of Orthodox Christianity at a time when other Christian churches have undergone great innovations are many, but it is too easy, particularly in a culture permeated with residual puritanism, to dismiss the beauty of its ritual and ornament as an empty appeal to the senses. The icons, those works of liturgical art so despised in the 19th and early 20th centuries have, in the past fifty or so years attained the place in art history they deserved, irrespective of their ancillary nature in Orthodox worship. There is the liturgy, which should be foreign to people who avoid the formal in everything from dress, behavior, expression, and thought, but which seems to exercise an awesome appeal to the converts, some from traditions that avoid or even suspect ritual.

Some converts must overcome their own suspicions of icons and incense and vestments and golden objects. If they come from the Protestant tradition, they become conscious of the iconoclastic elements in their background. They must adjust to a human Christ, One with a mother. To follow the Evangelical Orthodox Bishop, Gordon Walker, in his recounting of the realization that liturgy and sacraments were organic to the Church from Her very institution, and that the Orthodox doctrines concerning Mary and icons were not only defensible but logical as well, since they proceeded from the Incarnation of Christ, is to be reminded that Orthodoxy in America will be a tribal religion only temporarily, and that the Church's future is assured. "And as for the danger of worshipping the icon," says this son of iconoclasm, "I no more mistake it for the one it pictures than I mistake the pictures in my wallet for my loved ones." Though we do not know whether or not the Evangelical Orthodox Church will ultimately achieve Patriarchal oversight and acceptance as one of the Canonical Orthodox Churches of America, Bishop Walker's contribution is nevertheless a powerful testimony of the appeal of Orthodoxy.

Others, like Maria King, demanded a moral and ecclesiastical rigor she perceived was lost in other Christian churches. There was no fear, however, that this rigor, since it unlocked the resources of piety and Patristic thought cherished in Orthodox Christianity, was to be a negative force. On the contrary, Orthodoxy highlighted the inadequacy of the social gospel and utopianism for Father John Morris, who felt dissatisfied with the simplistic beliefs of enthusiasm, on one hand, and the tolerance for innovation, represented by the ordination of women and watered down doctrine that are products of liberalism, on the other. The efforts to "demythologize the Scriptures, (to) desacralize the liturgy, and (to) psychoanalyze the saints," Father Paul O'Callaghan found, had undermined many Christian traditions to the point that "faith (had) to be constantly defended *internally*" making it difficult for worshippers to place their emphasis on "living" their faith. The decisions of Maria King and Fathers John Morris and Paul O'Callaghan to enter the Orthodox Church were forced, in large part, because of the Episcopal Church's ordination of women.

Father Tom Avramis, the only convert with ethnic roots in Orthodox culture, views himself as a "prodigal" who found his way back to the Orthodox Church by taking the same path as the others, the long, hard path of thought and feeling. Like Bishop Gordon Walker, he proceeded through Campus Crusade for Christ, but for him the questioning of all authority had a strong emotional component, since as a young college student he had rejected the Church's claims for Scripture. His essay is perhaps the most direct confrontation between what he perceived were the differing claims of the Bible and Church Tradition. But the confrontation existed in himself, not in the Church, and when he began to study the Bible from the perspective of Holy Tradition, he saw that "the Bible was originally oral tradition until it was written down" and accepted as Sacred Canon at the Third Ecumenical Council.

"From my own past," Bishop Gordon Walker states,

the very word 'eucharist' evoked images of a dead church bound by
dead tradition and a theology of salvation by works instead of grace. I
had no concept of grace actually flowing through the physical means of
Baptism or the Eucharist. In fact, I was anti-sacramental, being certain
that those who believed in sacramental theology denied the grace of God
and Holy Scripture.

Not realizing it, I held a purely cerebral and rationalistic view of
faith and grace. I perceived that primarily through the preaching of the
word of God (the Bible) God's grace was somehow beamed into our
hearts and lives. Thus, my doctrine of salvation depended entirely on a
person's I.Q. If he didn't have the intellectual capacity to understand
and believe, then his only hope (which I believed was assured) was that
God's grace covered him anyway.

To what do we owe the strong interest in Orthodox Christianity and the tangible growth of the Church? To the assembly
of Fathers, of course, those Beacons of the early, formative years
of Christianity, who guided and instructed and stabilized the
Church. It is the intellectual heritage provided by Patristic
thought that has given, and will continue to give, Orthodoxy the
power to outlast the innovations. But it is also the tenacity and
steadfastness by which the doctrines and way of life have been
retained and maintained by Orthodox people that provides the
convert with a sense of "being closer to God," as Maria King
states. "It is ancient. I feel like we are holding hands with
Christians down through the ages and are worshipping God
together with them." Father John Morris finds that "Orthodoxy
has preserved (the) Faith through persecution by ancient Rome,
Islam, the Turks, and contemporary Communism and will not
abandon its Faith to embrace the ever-changing fads of modern
liberal theology."

But this resistance to change has a less attractive by-product, and an introduction to the collection of essays in *Journeys to Orthodoxy* would not be complete without a brief
mention of ethnicism in the Church. The topic is dealt with
directly by many and alluded to by all. Most were "welcomed
with remarkable affection" by priests and parishes, but one was
told frankly "You are Western, we are Eastern. We think differently. . .You would feel out of place and lonely. It is better that
you stay (in your own Church)." This prediction of loneliness,
however, turned out to be untrue, for Maria King discovered that
"the Greek community (was) wonderful to me", making "me
feel welcome from the beginning."

11

For Father Gregory Wingenbach and his wife, who like many others have experienced a joint conversion experience, the decision of the 1970 Archdiocesan Clergy-Laity Congress to allow local conditions to determine the extent of English in the liturgy may have presaged a relaxation in the ethnic exclusivity that characterized many Greek Orthodox communities, but the feeling of being a *xenos* in the parish was, he felt, hard to avoid. Yet, the obstacle of pervasive ethnicism, though less imposing when actual contact is made with Orthodox, still exists, as Father Paul O'Callaghan found, and may create in the convert "the feeling that he/she can never completely belong in the Orthodox family." Father John Morris, on the other hand, found his pride in his own British heritage to be an initial block to his acceptance of Orthodoxy.

> Others refuse to overcome their own ethno-centrism and . . . to consider seriously the case for a religion considered 'foreign' by many Americans. Although some actually recognize the truth of Orthodoxy, they cannot liberate themselves from their own ethnic prejudices to embrace Orthodoxy. Indeed some are so devoted to American ethnicism that they refuse to recognize the legitimate need of most Orthodox churches to use some foreign languages during the worship to minister to the many foreign-born Orthodox Christians in America.

Some contributors feel pride in their American heritage and are impatient at what they perceive is the glacial pace with which Orthodoxy is Americanizing. Father Gregory Wingenbach, recalling how it was to grow up under nativist suspicions of his German-American background and Roman Catholic affiliation, warns that the defensiveness of the birthright Orthodox toward the convert may render them unable "to live up to our Church's Great Commission". Most seem to find that the ethnic element in Orthodoxy has its benefits, though all by and large seem to agree that it has taken them some time to adjust to it. Finally, Father John Morris provides a warning of his own: many converts to Orthodoxy, he writes, "abandon their 'Western' patterns of thought with great difficulty, if at all . . . and . . . try to pick and choose what aspects of The Faith they will accept."

But there is probably a regional and jurisdictional factor to the openness with which a convert is accepted into the Orthodox family of worshippers. And it also seems to be a matter of time before the issue is either resolved or ceases to be a problem.

Pilgrimage to Freedom

by Father Anthony Scott

In the autobiographical account of C. S. Lewis's own conversion *Surprised by Joy,* he writes of a certain longing, in German, a "Sehnsucht" which draws him ever onward toward Christ. He believed this "Sehnsucht" to be the foretaste of joy. This longing manifested itself to him in various forms at different ages of his life. As a child it was the distant, remote "greenness" of particular hills. Later it was the appeal of heroism and nobility in Norse mythology and all things "northern". Then it was the romance of Wagnerian music. Finally he is "surprised by joy" in a completely unexpected manner.

In writing this statement of my own conversion to Christ and my subsequent embrace of Christ in the Orthodox Church, I will attempt to describe a persistent inner prompting of my own life which always made its presence felt in varying forms at different times. For C. S. Lewis, it was a certain nostalgia or longing. For me, it was the desire for personal freedom — that inexpressible and ineffable joy of life by which all experiences are measured. It is only since I have entered into the communion of the Orthodox Church that I have felt the complete fulfillment of this life-long yearning. Following is the account of one person's quest and final discovery of personal, spiritual freedom.

Until the age of 12 my experience of the supernatural was limited to a few awkward words of prayer stammered by my father on Thanksgiving Day. During these I remained distracted, for I always fixed one wary eye on my three brothers to be sure that they did not grab the dressing before I did, and one keen eye on the enormous and tantalizing fowl resting on the platter before me. To be sure, as a family we made the requisite pilgrimages to church on the two high holy days of the year — Christmas and Easter. Any church would do, provided it was not the "Popish" one. My formal religious education consisted of one or two years of occasional attendance at a neighborhood church Sunday school while my parents remained at home. We did observe with great devotion and profound attention to detail the celebration of two saint's feastdays in the American civil calendar of religion: Santa Claus and the Easter Bunny.

The only Sunday morning rituals practiced in the Scott family household during those early years consisted of reading the funny papers and watching the distinctly second class variety of cartoons which appeared on television on that day. The only experience which I can now remember that simulated the reverential occurred on a daily basis on the Air Force bases on which I was raised. At a certain time every afternoon all movement came to a halt, everyone faced the flag, and patriotically placed his hand upon his heart while the bugler sounded retreat as the flag was lowered.

At the age of 12 a profound event occurred in this otherwise perfectly normal secular American family. In 1961 my father experienced an authentic religious conversion. It was a genuine "Saul knocked from his horse" personal encounter with Jesus Christ. Upon my father descended a palpable sense of peace and quietude which I had never observed before. This experience and its subsequent impact upon the family was the beginning of my own experience of Christ.

Several years before, my mother had suffered a mental breakdown attributed to acute chronic depression and schizophrenia. In the 1950's victims of those diseases were normally institutionalized because therapeutic mood-altering drugs were not commonly available. The monstrous hospital bills, the loss of a spouse, and the raising of four boys, ages four through twelve, resulted in severe and unmanageable stress upon my father, who had spent a great deal of his life pridefully maintaining his independence and self-sufficiency. His capitulation to Christ was complete. I distinctly remember that prior to my father's conversion he gambled, drank, smoked, and swore with a robust enthusiasm. Following his conversion, these vices mysteriously evaporated.

My father had lived a vividly colorful life and like the famous St. Augustine now felt a compelling attraction to demanding and austere moral rigorism. His denomination of choice was Southern Baptist fundamentalism. Here was a bare bones form of Christianity that a person convinced of his own

14

utter sinfulness and the total sovereignty of God could gnaw and crunch with satisfaction.

From a religious life that could best be described as aimless and occasional, we were suddenly thrust into a religious life which could be described as relentless and demanding. What now ensued was an intensive exposure to the vigorous proclamation of radical Protestantism. Virtually overnight, all four children were attending church school and worship services every Sunday. My older brother and I were enrolled in confirmation classes and were duly baptized one year later. The three oldest sons and my father began to usher every Sunday during the worship services. One particular summer I was sent to church camp to receive the benefits of day-long religious education for a two-week period.

As I began to understand the teachings of Christ at the very impressionable age of twelve, I learned that I was utterly depraved as a person. I discovered that the incredibly painful and bloody crucifixion of Christ had somehow taken away my depravity. (Secretly however, I knew that I was still depraved, and feared for my salvation. Why else would a "saved person" have such a graphic and original imagination concerning members of the opposite sex?) I was especially attentive to the sermons which spoke of the everlasting torment of sinners in Hell. Yet I was a clever twelve year-old and figured out that God had a secret master plan for my life which I was to attempt to decipher. The code book for the unravelling of this mystery was the Bible. Tragically, I found the Bible far more complex than any school textbook and infinitely more boring. Salvation seemed beyond one such as I. During this time I also learned that Catholics had perverted the teachings of Christ, establishing an anti-Christ in Rome, worshipped idols, made a supernatural goddess of the Virgin Mary, and cannibalistically devoured the Body and Blood of Christ.

One Sunday I arrived at the Air Force base chapel earlier than usual to see an inexperienced chaplain's assistant pull a wrong cord which, to my utter horror, removed the flat, plain cross which we used in our Baptist service, replacing it with an agonizing Christ affixed to an ornate crucifix which was used in the Catholic service. I was scandalized by this experience because

15

the various chapels and Baptist churches which I had attended up to that point were completely devoid of any form of decoration or religious ornamentation. They had bleached, white oak walls, monochromatic windows, and uncushioned pews. A central and prominent podium was the only focal point for the wandering eyes of a curious adolescent. From this pulpit sermons would roll down like thunder from the heights of Sinai.

For all of its limitations, this distinctly American expression of radical Protestantism brought me into my first tantalizing contact with personal freedom. It was in that church and among those fundamentalists that I first witnessed the sincere and humble faith of believers. These people were somehow in communication with some entity outside of themselves — some mysterious Transcendance that gave to them a sense of joy. Most importantly, I saw this in my father's transformation, but also in the various pastors who occupied the pulpit of our church. Each seemed to be a convinced and sincere follower of Christ. I was deaf to their entreaties then. If I met them now, or perhaps better to say, *when* I meet them again, I shall humbly thank them for their ministrations on my behalf and the preliminary encounter with freedom which they gave to me.

As long as I lived in the quiet backwaters of Randolph Air Force Base in San Antonio, Texas I could survive the firestorm of Southern Baptist country preaching. I felt frightened. I felt sinful. I felt condemned. Above all, I felt guilty. Yet I endured. I was like the man poised above a deep chasm: one foot on the assurance of salvation, one foot on the certitude of condemnation. This spiritual impasse was resolved for me, however, in 1965.

In that year my father retired from the Air Force and our family moved to the San Francisco Bay Area. Ironically, he became the manager of a night club which featured emerging rock talent. He found this job by looking up the nearest Southern Baptist church in the yellow pages, visiting the pastor, and asking for help to find a job. A non-believing husband of one of the members of that church owned the nightclub and gave my father a job.

I immediately began work as a dishwasher in a restaurant adjoining the nightclub. In the furthermost corner of the kitchen was a dark alcove where the timeclock could be found. Here also was the nightclub's emergency exit, which passed into the kitchen. One could just see through a crack in the door into the strange and wonderful world beyond. Busboy trays of dishes would accumulate under the steam nozzle, while I would quietly disappear to the back of the kitchen to watch the frenzied dancers through my secret portal and dream of the possibilities of life. Although only half of the stage and the merest slice of dance-floor was visible, with each driving beat of the bass guitar, small amounts of Protestant fundamentalism would ebb through the crack to be dissipated by the powerful vision beyond. I was dazzled. I was captivated. I was transfixed. This vision spoke to my blood. Here was something which promised to take me out of myself. Here were all the marvelous seductions of the world: sensuous, voluptuous, luxurious. In a few brief months I was transmogrified in my imagination from an obedient, although frightened Southern Baptist, to a lady-killing, liquor-swilling, footloose-dancing, denizen of the San Franciscan underground. I was fifteen years old.

Unknowingly, I had stumbled upon the parody of bodily freedom, a shadow of the actual feasting of the faithful which occurs at the Messianic Banquet. Here were the passions: a promising escape to sensual oblivion. This discovery of eros signalled the beginning of another conflict. On one side existed the mysterious though remote spiritual freedom which emanated from believers whom I had known, and on the other side was the tantalizing parody of freedom which was offered in erotica. Until my entrance into Orthodoxy, the quandry remained unresolved.

However, this world was only the secret life of my own imagination. For a period of two years my public life still consisted of regular Sunday school and church attendance, Sunday evening youth meetings, and occasional weekend retreats. One of the training exercises which we undertook on Sunday evenings was particularly characteristic of the Southern Baptist militaristic confession of Christianity. The youth were lined up all in a row with their Bibles at their sides. Orders were given.

"Attention!"

We stood straight as possible.

"Present arms!"

We all held our Bibles open in front of us.

"Seek verse!"

Each one madly thumbed through his Bible, seeking to be the first to find the Bible verse. As the verse was found, each person would step forward in turn. The first to come forward was given the honor of reading the verse aloud. Humiliated, I always stepped forward third or fourth, pretending that I had found the passage. I covered my embarrassment with a shrug and a joke. Whereas the other young people had long since learned the order of the books of the Bible, I still required the use of the table of contents.

On Sunday mornings, loud and long (never less than 45 minutes) sermons were given condemning the evils of dancing, card-playing, swearing, dirty books and Madison Avenue advertising. One can imagine how these lengthy Sunday sermons impacted a seventeen year-old who had just spent the previous night at Filmore West dancing under the strobe lights to Santana, Janis Joplin, and Jimi Hendrix, while being stoned on a pharmacy of drugs. After numerous family fights, both my older brother and I were excused from church attendance. Thus began the inevitable and visible manifestation of the internal headlong flight from the Church, Christianity, and God which had begun two years previously.

I launched an epic four-year journey, an exhilarating and fragrant plunge into the spice box of life. I was Odysseus journeying on his many magical adventures when I hitchhiked around California. I was the romantic poet William Wordsworth as I climbed snowclad Telescope Peak in Death Valley, seeing life as I had never seen it before.

There was a time when meadow, grove, and stream
The earth, and every common sight,
　　To me did seem
　　Apparelled in celestial light,
The glory and freshness of a dream.

I was Walt Whitman singing the body electric — *The Song Of Myself.* I was John Muir surveying "The Range of Light" of the High Sierra on wilderness backpacking treks. I was "Lucy in the Sky with Diamonds" as I tasted every California drug. I was Eldridge Cleaver, as I closed ranks with my generation against the Vietnam War. I was Allen Ginsberg when I lived in the

Haight-Ashbury. I was the *Steppenwolf* of Herman Hesse, the *One-Dimensional Man* of Herbert Marcuse, Dimitri of *Brother's Karamazov*. I was on the loose and had determined a course of reckless adventure.

Regretfully, excitement is a poor substitute for true freedom. For all excitement, all eroticism, all bodily pleasures repeated often enough, eventually become both familiar and boring. I sought personal liberation, but I found confusion. One truth only did I learn about freedom during those years. I came to believe that every man possessed free choice. Up to this point in my life, my actions had been largely determined by either the moral rigorism of my father's church or my own carnal rebellion against this rigorism. I began to believe that I myself could determine my path through life.

I spent one summer traveling through Mexico. Two particular events occurred in Mexico which were crucial to my later conversion to Christianity. In Taxco I chanced upon a group of blues musicians who were also traveling in Mexico. One of them was a Catholic Christian — a newly converted, very sincere, and compassionate Catholic Christian. He was one of the first evangelists of that phenomenon called the Jesus Movement that was to sweep across California within the next year. I felt that it was my duty to explain to him the obvious errors of his thinking. I employed every stratagem and rhetorical device. I could not dissuade him from his faith. In fact, he began to effectively and charitably refute my own flimsy and inconsistent arguments. I quickly sought the refuge of the ignorant and insecure: petulance and resentment.

One day we were eating a simple meal of chicken soup and tortillas. A common beggar, obviously a widow, for she was attired in black dress and scarf, stood at a kitchen door patiently watching us eat. The Christian turned to me and asked "Should we invite her to eat with us?" I lifted my head, looked into her eyes, and was forced to look away. It was one of those extremely rare experiences that one knows will be carried even to the deathbed, for in that one moment all boundaries of time and space had been obliterated. I had looked directly into the eyes of Jesus Christ. I snapped my head downward and shook it vigorously from side to side. I lied, "She's only a beggar. Mexico is filled with them." I would not invite the Christ to dine at my table. It has now been seventeen years since that afternoon and I still remember with startling clarity the expression of those eyes — infinitely patient, infinitely caring, infinitely accepting. Once or twice since that time, I have seen the same eyes in icons of uncommon tenderness.

I formally became a Christian on August 12, 1968, sometime between 11:00 P.M. and 12:00 A.M. on an empty stretch of beach south of Half Moon Bay in California. Some Orthodox Christians, born and baptized into the Church, respond with skepticism to such a statement. Nevertheless, it is possible for me to identify a particular point in time at which I can say that I accepted the Lordship of Jesus Christ and the sovereignty of Father, Son, and Holy Spirit. That is to say, there was a specific moment when I accepted the existence of a transcendent Being and that I identified this Being with the Jewish rabbi who was known as Jesus of Nazareth.

Young people in California frequently get in their cars late at night and drive to the beach to be alone. It is a time to question, a time to seek, a time to dream, a time to ask eternal questions of life. Standing on the shores of the largest ocean in the world, listening to the roar and the *shhh* of the waves on the sand, looking at the vault of heaven, smelling the primal fragrance of the sea, feeling the wind and spray on the face, one gains appropriate perspective, appropriate distance from commonality. One is shocked when answers to eternal questions are shouted back from the cosmos.

While driving to the beach, I had come to a conclusion. The answer to the quest for freedom did not lie outside of me in the pursuit of pleasure or in the discovery of some exotic philosophy. The answer was to be found somewhere deep within myself. I had never felt so determined to resolve an issue before. As I walked on the beach, I steadied myself for the inward journey. I lay on the sand, stared into the wheel of the galaxy, and for the first time permitted the personal philosophy which I had been developing since abandoning the Christianity of my youth to proceed to its logical conclusion. On that particular evening, the stars seemed painfully cold, the heavens frighteningly vacuous.

I allowed myself to feel completely alone in the universe. The heavens are empty, I told myself. They are completely devoid of any supernatural entity. I shall always be alone, separated from others by the walls of the body. I will never be more than a simple acquaintance to any other person, an intermittent companion, sometimes present, more frequently absent. Sharing my life with another person will be utterly futile. For the duration of my life I will be bound within the confines of my own ego, limited to the meager and often unpleasant resources of my own mind.

I allowed my thoughts to flow to the inevitable conclusion of my life. A memory awakened which had remained quietly sleeping within my mind for many years. I was living in Denver. I must have been five or six years old. I recall waiting for a bus with other children. A whiff of extremely unpleasant odor stabbed my nose. A trashy drainage ditch was not more than ten feet away. I walked over to the ditch and looked down. At first I did not understand what I looked upon. I had never seen anything quite like it before. It seemed to be a sleeping dog, although I had never seen a dog sleeping in such an awkward position before. I realized that it could not be sleeping, though, because it had its teeth bared as though it were smiling, or perhaps growling. I bent over and looked a little closer. The entire surface of the animal was rippling with little white worms. They were in its eyes, its mouth, its ears. An incredibly powerful wave of stench arose. I turned away in horror and nausea, having looked upon the ancient enemy of man for the first time.

Now, peering into the heavens and feeling that they were terribly empty, I knew with certitude that this was also to be my destiny. Some day I too would lie in the grave with that dog and become that same banquet for maggots and erupt that same nauseating stench. I began to picture myself as the dog in the ditch. It was my eyes, my mouth, my ears that were covered with the little white worms. There was someone else who was gazing upon my corpse. I began to question: was this to be the final result of my life? As de Maupassant had written: "After a stupid life, a stupid death." I despaired.

Once I had lain for three days in a $1 room in Oaxaca, Mexico, incapacitated with amoebic dysentery. I was 2,000 miles from anyone I knew. I spoke but half a dozen words of Spanish. I did not have the meager strength needed to wash myself or to change the sheet of the bed on which I lay. Yet I would gladly have exchanged the despair and hopelessness of those three days and nights with the absolute despair and utter hopelessness of that one hour.

Another childhood memory arose. Now I was in Kansas City in 1957. A terrifying and monstrous tornado was thundering toward our house. Cars and refrigerators were flying through the air. I imagined that I was sucked up inside this tornado. Only now the tornado was composed of all the demons of hell, whirling and swirling about me. It seemed as though I had torn open the stomach of hell. I feared for my sanity. Somewhere on the edge of this hellish vortex, I perceived a single flame, as of a candle. It appeared to be miles distant. It was the only constant in my apocalyptic nightmare. I focused upon the flame and would not allow my eyes to stray from it. I surprised myself by praying. I begged this flame to become brighter, clearer, closer. Gradually, as it waxed in intensity, I recognized in it the face of Christ, His eyes brimming with tears. It was He Who had come to save me from my own foolishness.

The torment may have lasted as long as several hours. From beginning to end I clung tenaciously to the face of Christ in the flame. For this reason I accepted the name of St. Anthony of the Desert when I became Orthodox, as he also had suffered torturous visitations of the dancing devils of hell. Locked in an ancient Egyptian cemetery for many years, he was assaulted by all manner of satanic fiends. Like St. Anthony, I knew that my only hope was to fall at the feet of Christ in adoration and worship.

Call it by any name — psychosis, delusion, madness. For me, it will always remain the horror of genuine, Biblical, demonic possession. For two years following that night, for varying lengths of time, I suffered as the Gerasene demoniac living among the tombs, possessed by a legion of unclean spirits. During that time, over and over again, I diligently read and reread the New Testament. I prayed six or seven times daily. I worshipped in church every Sunday. I felt compelled to follow this regimen, for whenever I faltered in any of the tasks the devils would return. These activities seemed to be the only alternative to hell.

As I now try to recall that first meeting with Christ, and His rather dramatic intervention into my life, my most powerful remembrance is one of unconditional love and acceptance. I had once been gifted with a red-letter, imitation, white leather Bible for perfect Sunday School attendance. In those first few days of my meeting with Christ I received immeasurable comfort in thumbing through this Bible to find the incredibly naive and sentimental pictures of Jesus in His ministry. In one He was healing the blind man, in one He was forgiving the thief, in one He was blessing the children. In turn, I became each recipient of His love; blind man, thief, and child. In Christ I experienced infinite love, complete forgiveness, and total acceptance. In that hour on that remote California beach, the Ancient of Days and Father of Lights had extended His hand and delicately blessed me with His presence.

The demonic possessions ended quite unexpectedly one night after I had been awakened from a sweaty and fitful sleep. Three demons were present in the room sniggering at my sufferings. These particular demons were well known to me. With all the conviction that I could summon, I shouted in a loud voice "In the name of Jesus Christ, I command you to depart and never to return!" I immediately fell into the sweetest and deepest sleep I had enjoyed in two years. Since that time I have never been troubled by visitations of demons in this form. True, I suffer the same temptations as all men. And like all men born of Adam, save One, I too am a sinner. Yet ever since that time the demons have never returned to torture me.

For years I had been enslaved by either the fear of my childhood religion, or the excesses of my prodigal youth, or the persecutions of the demons, or the limitations of my own intellect. I had always desired a freedom which would take me out of myself and yet somehow put me back into myself. Ironically, with this radically new discovery in Christ, I lost all interest in personal freedom. I prepared myself to become the abject slave of the Messiah Jesus of Nazareth. I had been carried out of the mouth of Hell and would never forget the One who had lifted me. The New Testament speaks of the Church as the dwelling place of Christ. Therefore, I would begin a new quest. I would search for the Church of the New Testament. Surely it continued to exist, for Christ would not abandon the Church which He had established, about which He promised "the gates of hell would not prevail". When I found it, I would surrender to the presence of Christ within it.

I began with what was familiar to me. I attended various meetings of Protestant, para-ecclesiological campus ministries: Inter-Varsity Christian Fellowship, Campus Crusade, and a phenomenon unique to Berkeley, the Christian World Liberation Front. Although I was impressed with the sincerity and zeal of the members of these particular groups, I always left the meetings with a sense of being incomplete. These Christians functioned under a common basic supposition. They seemed to believe that the One, Holy, Catholic, and Apostolic Church of Christ was not physically visible. For them it was invisible and existed only by faith. Some believed that each church possessed one aspect of the One, True Church of Christ. Therefore, if it were possible to combine all of the churches together, the end result would be the one Church of Christ. Never mind the contradictions of belief and practice which existed among these churches. This common supposition was a necessary one for Christians, who centuries before had separated from the historical, Apostolic Church of Christ. I was convinced, however, that this Church must still exist somewhere, although I had no idea where to find it.

I began a methodical search. I enrolled in New Testament classes. I attended not less than fifteen different churches. I read not less than fifty books and engaged in dialogue with a dozen different ministers, always searching, looking, hoping to find the "pearl of great price" — the Bride and Body of Christ. Perhaps it was the relativism of the day or of the atmosphere of Berkeley in the late 1960's, but not one of these ministers dared to believe or to teach me that I had found the One, True Church, not even the Catholic priests of the Newman Center!

It was far more than this lack of conviction which prompted me to search beyond the Western Church. In whatever group or church I attended during this time, I consistently encountered several disconcerting tendencies. These were an elaborate and legalistic concern with moral behavior, an extremely pessimistic perspective of human nature, and an atmosphere of guilt. I did not realize until my later theological studies that these elements were 'built into the system' of Western Christianity. I was also uncomfortable with the secularism, humanism, and relativism of the West (though I did not yet know the names of these spiritual afflictions). Lastly, I made the startling discovery

24

that Catholics and Protestants were still fighting the bitter internecine war of the Reformation and Counter-Reformation, ecumenical posturing notwithstanding.

In addition to the above-listed elements which had been built into Western Christianity through historical development, the bequest of the radical Reformers specifically included a renunciation of sacred materialism, a denial of sacramental realism, separation from the righteous dead in Christ, only partial communion with the Body of Believers, the purging of the veneration of the Virgin Mary, an extremely narrow appreciation of beauty and majesty, and a 1500 year Rip van Winkle time lapse of Church history. I began to fear that the choice fell between the excessive individualism of the Reformation churches or the surrender of conscience to Roman Catholic juridical legalism. Orthodoxy came to me as a thief in the night, completely unheralded and unexpected.

While a student at Berkeley, I would occasionally return home for the weekend. My younger brother, who still lived at home, had become a Christian several years before and had begun his own search for the Bride of Christ. Later, he was to become a monk of the Orthodox Church and also a deacon. On one of these weekends he invited me to go to a church with him which he had attended a few times before. It was an Orthodox Church in the Antiochian Archdiocese.

The membership of the church was composed primarily of disenchanted former Episcopalians who had migrated en masse to the Orthodox Church. There were perhaps one hundred total members of the parish. The nave could not have been larger than 40' x 60'. The icons had been written* by someone in the parish. The priest lived in a one bedroom apartment adjoining the sanctuary. The parishioners had built the structure almost entirely with their own hands. The services were conducted completely in English. Here the paradox of the Nativity was re-enacted. Three kings came searching for the King of Kings and were surprised to find him in a stable. I had been searching for the great and glorious Church of the Apostles with banners flying and trumpeters announcing its presence. I had found a comple-

---

* *In Orthodox terminology, icons are "written," not drawn or painted.*

tely unimpressive little church off Magdalena Exit on Highway 280 in Los Altos, California.

I remember very clearly the first Liturgy I attended. Beyond the people was the iconostasis. Unearthly pictures of holy saints floated upon golden backgrounds, billows of exotic-smelling smoke poured from a censer ringing with bells. Candles flickered before icons, conveying life and movement. A priest, elaborately vested in garments of intricate and flowing designs, held paten of Body and chalice of Blood. The virginal, religious sensitivities of this former Southern Baptist were inundated. Never did I smell or hear or see or taste in the Kingdom of God until that moment. I felt like the celebrated ambassadors of St. Prince Vladimir of Russia who, after visiting Hagia Sophia in Constantinople, returned to report "We knew not whether we were in heaven or earth. For on earth there is no such splendor or such beauty, and we are at a loss to describe it. We know only that God dwells there among men . . . For we cannot forget that beauty."

A work day had been called for the next Saturday to paint the new hall. My brother and I came to help. We were greeted so warmly and cordially by the people and thanked so profusely for helping that we very quickly felt strong bonds of friendship with the community. On weekends while at home and during the summer I attended this church. While at school, I began to worship in a small Orthodox mission nearby.

I studied as a catechumen for one year. I read the standard primers on Orthodoxy: Schmemann's *For the Life of the World,* Ware's *Orthodox Church,* the anonymous *Way of a Pilgrim* and Bloom's *Beginning to Pray* and *God and Man.* I changed my form of personal prayer by employing the Jordanville *Prayer Book.* I learned to incorporate my body in worship: lighting candles, burning incense, venerating icons and making prostrations. A very active chapter of the Orthodox Christian Fellowship at U. C. Berkeley convened weekly. Our meetings often had forty people present. There were also retreats conducted by local Orthodox priests. At the conclusion of that year and only a few months before graduation, I was Confirmed, Confessed and Communed into the Orthodox Church.

Why did Orthodoxy speak to me? It offered a glorious sacred materialism without guilt. God became 'touchable'. Orthodox theologians wrote optimistically about the nature of man. Orthodoxy spoke with the voice of the Fathers of the Church. The liturgical life breathed timeless truths of man and God. The sacraments were in this world, revealing the world in its true meaning. And though it was never boasted or even publicly stated, Orthodox Christians knew that they lived in the Church which Christ had established. For the first time, I felt that the Church was no longer an entity upon which man imposed his own opinions, but rather the place in which the Life of Christ was glorified and revealed to the world.

I cannot explain why I chose to go to seminary immediately following entrance into the Church, except to say that Orthodoxy addressed my deepest need to experience Christ in a tangible and concrete manner. The more I immersed myself in the life of the Church, the more I entered into communion with Christ. It seemed logical that if I desired to experience Christ most fully in the Church, I should go to the place where this experience was intensified.

In August of 1971, with shoulder-length hair, one pair of faded, patched levis, a blue denim workshirt, and ten dollars, I stood on a freeway entrance ramp to Interstate 80 near Oakland, California and began to hitchhike to St. Vladimir's Seminary in New York. I carried an orange Denali backpack with *The Way of a Pilgrim* and a small paperback Bible carefully stored inside. I arrived ten days later at about 2:00 a.m. on a Sunday morning. Not wanting to wake anyone, I quietly went to sleep in the only readily available place, a couch in the ladies' restroom.

The next morning I was awakened by the bells summoning the community to the Liturgy. I washed as well as I could and began to walk to the chapel. On the stairs leading to the chapel I met Professor S. Verhovsky: Dean of Students and Provost. Although small of stature, 'The Professor', as he is called, can be quite imposing. Trained in European theological academies, he projected a rigid and formidable demeanor. Strictly formal, he was always carefully dressed in coat and tie. Staunch defender of the doctrines of the Church, he was quick to seize any uninformed statement of a student and logically, methodically, and dogmatically expose it for its obvious foolishness.

'The Professor' used a cane because he was afflicted with a recurrent and painful case of gout, and it was not difficult for me to pass by him on the stairs leading to the chapel. I heard a commanding voice, "Just a minute, young man. I wish to speak with you." I turned to look and met the stern, analytical eyes of 'The Professor'. With a bemused expression, he examined me with the careful manner of the dogmatician. "Young man, do you intend to become a student at this seminary?" Up until that moment I would have responded with an enthusiastic exclamation. Facing this obvious figure of authority, I began to feel uncertain of myself. I suppose I must have stammered a yes, because he asked me a second question. It was a question that immediately stripped away all artifice, something for which 'The Professor' was legendary. He lifted his cane, pointed it at me and asked, "Young man, why did you come to this seminary?" I replied, "Love brought me here." He paused and very slowly said, "You are welcome here, young man. Shall we go up to the Liturgy?"

In his famous autobiography, Thomas Merton described the moment he arrived to become a postulant at Our Lady of Gethsemani Abbey in rural Kentucky: "So brother Matthew locked the gate behind me, and I was enclosed in the four walls of my new freedom." This was precisely the description of my own beginning at seminary. We were now told when to awaken, when to work, when to go to class, and when to pray. The regimen was unfamiliar and difficult in the beginning. Libertine Berkeley was never like this. Yet the liturgical life and the community life confirmed to me in ways wonderful and marvelous all of the reasons why I had become Orthodox.

I had zealously pursued personal freedom for a decade. And although there had been glimpses and fleeting touches of it during that time, it had always appeared to be just beyond my grasp. The further I stretched forth my clasping hand, the further it receded. After I became a Christian, I abandoned this great hope and quest of my early life in exchange for slavery to Christ. Now, with no expectations or anticipations, I was gifted with this greatest hope and dream of my youth. The freedom for which I had always hungered was given to me without my asking for it. It was the freedom of the communal life of Christ experienced within the Church.

It was a freedom that seemed somehow familiar and yet absolutely fresh and unknown. It was not the intellectual 'eureka' that I had imagined it would be, nor even the liberation from some imprisonment. Freedom was much more like the joy and delight of a surprise meeting with someone whom one loves. I felt the strangeness and wide-eyed wonder of one who, after having first been a prodigal and then a slave in the house of the Master, is unexpectedly vested with the mantle of sonship.

In 1978, Fr. Alexander Schmemann was conducting a retreat in my parish. He was unquestionably the greatest liturgical scholar in the world. He had written learned treatises on virtually every significant liturgical question of our generation. He had been my dean and professor of Liturgical Theology at seminary. He had been my Father Confessor and spiritual guide. As one of his former students, I was painfully concerned with any possible lapses on my part in the rubrics of the services. I desired everything to be perfect. I was overcome with embarrassment when I discovered that I did not have the listing for the daily Gospel reading for the Divine Liturgy we were celebrating on that Saturday. What would he think of a priest and former student who had not even had the intelligence or foresight to research the particular Gospel reading for a Divine Liturgy? I was terrified. I must have appeared enormously nervous when I informed him of my lapse because he simply smiled and asked me, "Are we not free men? My dear Fr. Anthony, choose what you would like to read. The Sabbath was made for man not man for the Sabbath." Perhaps this simple illustration will provide a better explanation of freedom than what I have attempted to describe in my own conversion story, for though I always sought personal freedom, I believe that in a much more profound way the only completely Free One was always seeking me, patiently waiting to gift me with the freedom of life in Orthodoxy.

A Pilgrimage of Faith

by Father Paul O'Callaghan

A literal translation of the word "Orthodoxy" would be "pure glory." By the grace of God, I have come to know His true glory within the bosom of the Orthodox Church. This essay describes my experience.

I was raised in a faithful, devoted Roman Catholic home. Accordingly, I cannot remember a time when I did not know Christ or when prayer and worship were absent. Although I did indeed drift from my childhood faith later in life, when I returned to a committed Christianity, it was definitely a *return* to the Christian "roots" that had always existed deep in my soul. Thus, rather than a "journey to Christ," my particular spiritual journey might be called a "pilgrimage of faith."

Major changes in life, such as conversion to another religious tradition, do not occur in a vacuum. Such decisions occur within a context determined by interactions between one's personality, ethnic background, cultural environment, faith commitment, and historical experience. In my case, my journey to Orthodoxy was intimately tied to my experience of growing up as a Catholic from the late 1950's to the early 1970's. During this period, the Roman Church effectively demythologized the Scriptures, desacralized the Liturgy, and psychoanalyzed the Saints. I found eventually that I could neither identify with the old, legalistic, Pre-Vatican II Catholicism or the new, liberated, Post-Vatican II Catholicism. This led in the end to my positive affirmation of Orthodox Christianity. Thus, to understand the process of my conversion to Orthodoxy, it is necessary to also understand the developments that occurred in Roman Catholicism as I was growing up.

The decade of the 1960's was especially a period of turbulence and upheaval within the Catholic world. The Second Vatican Council not only promulgated radical reforms in liturgy and worship, but also was a major factor in revolutionizing the

Church's self-consciousness. As a result, the monolithic unity and ironclad discipline so characteristic of Tridentine Catholicism began to crumble. The Liturgical Movement, the renewal of biblical studies with the adoption of higher criticism, and the realization of the historically conditioned nature of the Church's existence prompted Catholic theologians to begin questioning what before had been unquestionable. What began as a long-overdue movement for renewal eventually commenced an erosion of Catholic consensus that persists to this day. Is the Pope really infallible? Is birth control permissible? Can homosexual practices be considered morally acceptable? The widely varying opinions on these and other important topics among Catholic theologians today are evidence enough of the drastic nature of the modern Catholic metamorphosis. Personally living through these changes had a serious effect on my spiritual development, as well as that of many of my contemporaries.

I was born in the early 1950's in the San Francisco suburb of Marin County. The largely Irish, Italian, and German concentration of Catholics in San Francisco was also reflected in the suburbs. Thus even Marin County boasted numerous Catholic parishes with well organized parochial schools and a local high school as well. These schools were mainly staffed by Dominican nuns whose convent was just down the street from my boyhood home.

As Catholics in that setting in the late 1950's and early 1960's, we possessed a strong sense of identity and distinctiveness. Even though I was a young child, I shared the bedrock conviction that we belonged to the "one true Church," that Jesus had established Peter as the first Pope, and that following the teachings of the Roman Church was the only sure way to heaven. In my mind, Protestants and "the Greeks" were looked upon with a mixture of disdain and curiosity. Wasn't it sufficiently obvious to them that the Roman Catholic Church was the only true Church?

In the second grade, I was lucky enough to be able to enter the local parochial school (there wasn't room for all of the applicants); I also made my "first Communion" that year. Of course, the only language that was heard in the Church at that time was Latin, the service being conducted according to the ancient Tridentine rite. But within several years, the changes began. First, a table was placed in front of the altar so that the priest could say mass facing the people. People were expected to take a more active role in the liturgy, and English began to be introduced into the service.

Most people seemed to react positively at first to the changes, although some (like my mother, a convert from Protestantism) began to worry about what was happening to the Church. However, it was undeniable that people were participating in the mass in a far more meaningful way. In earlier days, lay people would often pray the rosary or use other private devotions during mass since there was little or no way for them to participate. Now it seemed that people were actively worshipping together.

At the same time, changes were taking place outside the strictly liturgical sphere. For instance, in my early years in parochial school, we were taught that eating meat on Friday was a mortal sin. This meant that if you were to have a hamburger on Friday and die on Saturday without receiving the sacrament of penance, you would spend eternity in hell. Then one day one of the parish priests visited our classroom. The Church, he explained, had changed the rule forbidding meat on Fridays. It was no longer a law of the Church, no longer a mortal sin. The Church wanted us to make the sacrifice on our own, not out of fear of punishment.

That argument sounded reasonable enough at the time. But later, I was to ponder: How could something be a mortal sin one day, worthy of eternal damnation, and the next day not be a sin at all?

I entered the local Catholic high school in the late 1960's. Although I had been very pious as a young boy, by the time I entered high school I had become apathetic in my attitude towards religion. This had little to do with the changes in the Church, but was more the result of laziness, the neglect of daily prayer, and a typical youthful preoccupation with "having fun" and pleasure-seeking. It was my high-school experience, however, that would eventually prove pivotal in causing me to begin my pilgrimage to Orthodoxy.

During the late 1960's, radical changes began to take place in the social structure of the once-sleepy suburbs of Marin County. Although the San Francisco Bay Area was spared during the epidemic of race riots that afflicted other cities, there was constant agitation taking place across the Bay at the U.C. Berkeley campus. Also, a large number of the "hippies" from the Haight-Ashbury district of San Francisco began moving over to semi-rural Marin. Many young people, myself included, began to be affected by the "anti-establishment" behavior that was becoming prevalent. An attitude of rebelliousness and relentless questioning of authority spread among many youth. Although the majority remained "conformist," a large percentage of the students at Marin Catholic High School were seduced by the promise of easy freedom offered by "hippieism."

Needless to say, the anti-establishment fervor of the period was not conducive to appreciation for highly institutionalized and authoritarian forms of religion such as Roman Catholicism. Personally, I still believed in Jesus and the teachings of the Bible (of which I knew little), but the Church seemed all too human, all too fallible. A radical distinction existed in my mind between what Jesus had taught and the traditions of men embodied in the Church. Unfortunately, however, I knew next to nothing of what Jesus really did teach. My entire approach to religion was dictated by the secular philosophy I had adopted.

It was here that my teachers failed me. We studied the higher criticism of the Scriptures, but we never studied the Bible as the Word of God addressed to us. We pondered the complexities of ethical decision-making, but were not informed of the unfailing standards of God revealed in Scripture, the Fathers, and the Saints. In their eagerness to be sailing with the latest winds of doctrine, my instructors in religion ignored the firm foundation upon which genuine faith must be built. Consequently, I was only encouraged to continue a rebellious and sinful lifestyle.

Jesus once pointed out that a person who builds his house on shifting sands is headed for disaster (Mt.7: 26-27). This truth is clearly demonstrated by my experience in high school. One of the priests who instructed us in our faith ran off with the girls' physical education teacher. Another married a nun and left the Church. Others were saddled with severe drinking problems. Yet another had a seemingly unending preoccupation with scatological jokes. In addition, the vast majority of the nuns I had had as teachers in grammar school left the order by the time I graduated from high school. It was obviously easy to develop a cynical attitude in this situation.

During my last year in high school, I began to avoid going to mass on Sunday for the first time. I did so by deceiving my parents, for in a pious Catholic family such as mine to do so was unthinkable. At that point, I had completely drifted from the Church. But this was not to last for long.

Around the time I graduated, a new current was penetrating Marin County. The "Jesus Movement" had arrived. Young people were on street corners and college campuses preaching out of Bibles. Ex-hippies and radicals were espousing Jesus Christ as the only true way to freedom and authentic transformation. The question "Have you accepted Jesus into your heart?" was constantly being asked. Bible study groups, street ministries, and Christian coffee houses sprang up everywhere almost over-night.

At first, I ridiculed the "Jesus freaks" along with my friends. But I soon found as I listened to their message that a burning sense of its truth inflamed my soul. At the same time, however, I was developing an interest in Yoga and Eastern Mysticism. A deep desire to encounter the living God encompassed me. I began to attend local youth Bible Studies and searched deeply for spiritual truth. Soon thereafter, my heart became convinced: Jesus Christ is the Way, the Truth, and the Life, the only way to the Father. With this realization came the conversion of my life. I committed myself totally to Christ and His Gospel.

Although I did not realize it at first, the theology and piety of the Jesus movement were deeply evangelical Protestant. Eventually, however, it became apparent that there was a fundamental conflict between this evangelicalism and my inherently Catholic approach to Christianity. This conflict was not simply on the level of ideas but existed in my inner experience of truth. Since my conversion, I had gained a renewed appreciation not only of Scripture and its great themes but of the sacramental life and the saints as well. Thus I could neither fully identify with the Jesus movement or the Roman Church. Committed to Christ as I was, I nonetheless experienced an inner "schizophrenia" in my spiritual life.

In the meantime, I changed my major in college from psychology to religious studies. I began to feel a strong urge to enter the ministry and preach the gospel. How and where, I did not know. I attended various churches and plunged deeply into the study of theology. In my theological research, however, I ran up against the same Protestant-Roman Catholic dilemma. Yet my studies gradually led to one sure conclusion: The Roman Catholic Church had consistently been responsible for dubious innovations in theology and spirituality, and Protestantism existed as a reaction against Romanism. Thus, neither tradition evidenced catholic fullness.

Only at this point did Orthodoxy suggest itself. I knew nothing of the Eastern Church at this time, as my Catholic educators had always portrayed Orthodoxy as sort of a Roman Catholicism without the Pope. But what a revelation the discovery of true Orthodoxy would be!

Our college library contained a small section of books on the Orthodox Church. Here I found my first real introduction to the Church. I avidly read the classics by Timothy Ware, Ernst Benz, and Nicholas Zernov. But it was Professor Fedetov's *Treasury of Russian Spirituality* that provided the living touch of the Spirit which can be the only true communicator of Orthodoxy. Reading selections from Fr. John of Kronstadt's "My Life in Christ" and St. Seraphim's "Conversation" revealed a Christianity that was at once catholic and evangelical in the best sense of those terms. Here was a wholeness that transcended traditional Roman-Protestant debates from a perspective of unbroken Spirit-bearing tradition.

Orthodoxy, I learned, retained ancient customs such as fasting on Fridays without, however, attaching the legal strictures to them that Roman Catholicism had. The sacraments were emphasized in a new and original way that did not degenerate into mere sacramentalism. The Orthodox Saints stressed faith in Christ and the life in the Spirit in a manner that excelled the best in evangelical "personal religion". Unbiblical Roman doctrines and practices were unknown or rejected. To summarize, Orthodoxy showed itself to retain that catholic fullness that Christ and the Apostles had originally bequeathed to the Church.

While continuing my studies, I naturally became curious about Orthodox worship. Books I had attempted to read on the subject were frankly incomprehensible, due to the unique vocabulary they contained. Thus, the next logical step for me was to begin to attend Orthodox services.

I can vividly remember my initial visits to Orthodox Churches. Although I was somewhat mystified about what was going on, I was impressed deeply by the profound sense of the sacred, the deep intensity of the Orthodox Liturgy. I had grown sick of the pathetic attempts of many Roman Catholic priests to turn the mass into something casual or even "fun." In the Orthodox services, one knew that a holy God was being worshipped. The music was elevating instead of banal, the architecture uplifting instead of dull. The many icons gave the impression that the worshipping congregation was indeed of one company with the angels and saints in the heavenly kingdom. I realized that there was a cohesive unity between Orthodox theology, spirituality, and worship. There was also a strong sense of continuity in the liturgy between the time of Christ and the modern era. It was something ancient and venerable, not a product of the "secular 60's," which had so strongly flavored the revised Roman rite. The continuity felt in worship was manifest in theology and spirituality as well. These realizations prompted me to delve deeper into the study of Orthodoxy, as well as to begin to visit Orthodox churches on a more frequent basis.

Within the period of about a year, I felt that I wanted to convert to Orthodoxy, yet I hesitated. I had been attending an Episcopal Church and was still not quite clear in my religious convictions. My background, training, and experience were all within the ethos of Western Christianity. And although I had been welcomed with friendliness in most of the Orthodox churches I had visited, there was a definite awareness in my mind of the "Easternness" of Orthodoxy. I realized that conversion would be a drastic step.

Coupled with these considerations were the questions raised by the fact that I felt strongly called to the ministry. What about the seemingly pervasive ethnicism so evident in Orthodox communities? Was it not absurd for an "outsider" even to consider serving in the Orthodox priesthood? Would I ever be accepted in an Orthodox community? Would I even be able to communicate effectively with people of a far different culture?

These questions seemed to indicate conclusive "no" answers. I decided to put Orthodoxy out of my mind and to continue worshipping within the comprehensive Anglican tradition. Many of the Episcopal priests I had known were lovers of

Orthodoxy; I felt comfortable with them and their congregations. I decided to prepare for the priesthood of the Episcopal Church.

Unfortunately, (or fortunately, as the case may be), soon after this decision the Episcopal Church entered into the most controversial and divisive period of its history. The Church resolved to ordain women to the priesthood and drastically revise the prayer-book. Little concern for Apostolic faith and practice was evident within the Church leadership. Liturgically, things seemed to be going the way of Roman Catholicism. Again the beacon light of Orthodoxy stood out clearly in an otherwise overpowering darkness. It seemed impossible to doubt that Orthodoxy could uniquely claim to be the One, Holy, Catholic, and Apostolic Church of Christ.

With a fresh sense of resolve and conviction, I decided to contact a local Orthodox pastor and share all my thoughts and concerns with him. To my deep surprise, he was immediately responsive, supportive, and understanding. After speaking with him several times, I was strongly encouraged to enter the Church and to study for the priesthood. He worked on my apprehensions until I felt confident about overcoming the "cultural gap" previously mentioned. He pledged to use his every influence with the bishop in my interest.

Needless to say, I was overwhelmed to be welcomed with such love and enthusiasm. It seemed as if God Himself was opening the doors for me. With great joy, I was chrismated into the faith. No, the concerns and apprehensions did not vanish overnight. I did feel a little odd in the midst of a community that was overwhelmingly Arabic in background. But again, I was received with an overwhelming warmth. I soon entered Holy Cross Greek Orthodox seminary and was ordained to the priesthood in 1979.

Although it might seem that my pilgrimage ended when I was chrismated, life in Christ never reaches a "goal" at which stasis is achieved. The Fathers teach that even in heaven our eternity will be one of unending growth in God. Thus, while in a certain sense my conversion put an end to a period of religious "searching," that conversion also merely expanded my spiritual horizons so as to make me conscious of new possibilities and opportunities. I realized that living the life of the kingdom of

God is inescapably challenging; simply belonging to the "true Church" would not insure my spiritual fruitfulness.

The positive values in Orthodoxy that led to my conversion are, I hope, now clear. Those things continue to be a source of spiritual strength. It is wonderful to belong to a faith-community where the faith does not have to be constantly defended *internally*, so that emphasis may be put on living it. In our confused age, it is essential for the Church to have the inner conviction to proclaim resolutely "Thus saith the Lord . . . ." The glory of Orthodoxy is that it can do so in a manner that is compelling to people of the modern era.

While the glories of the faith are especially evident to the convert, yet in some ways it remains difficult to be a committed convert within the Orthodox Church. The various cultural factors that originally held me back from converting are still very much present in most Orthodox communities. Thus, it is almost impossible to convert to Orthodoxy without at the same time "converting" to being Greek, Slavic, or Arabic. To do so in a literal sense is of course impossible, but having to integrate into a foreign ethnic cultural tradition is often difficult, and can lead to a consequent confusion in one's own sense of cultural identity. Coupled with this is the problem that a convert always seems to remain a "convert," something less than a "born Orthodox," and is often perceived as "different" or as an "outsider." Even more problematic is the attitude found among some Orthodox that Orthodoxy is almost "genetic." If you do not have the right ethnic pedigree, it is asked, how can you be Orthodox?

In this regard, I can remember a question once put to me by a young man before a wedding service. He asked me my name, and when I told him, he replied "How are you Orthodox? Shouldn't you be Catholic or Protestant?" Perhaps questions like these are in some sense perfectly natural given the realities of Orthodoxy in America today. However, they tend to give the "convert" the feeling that he/she can never completely belong in the Orthodox family.

Other and perhaps more dangerous pitfalls exist for the convert to Orthodoxy. Most converts tend to be well-educated in the faith, but a "bookish" approach to Orthodoxy can be disastrous in that it ignores the wide divergence between the theory of Orthodoxy and the actual realities of parish life. Orthodox theologians are somewhat responsible for this problem, since they tend to focus exclusively on mystical or purely theological aspects of the Church's life. In spite of all the talk about "incarnational theology," Orthodox writers often take an almost ethereal approach to the Church that can give a gross misimpression of the actual reality of Orthodoxy. Thus, our theologians have articulated a beautiful doctrine of the eucharistic nature of the Church, while at the same time in many Orthodox parishes no one over the age of two receives communion most Sundays of the year. A convert may also discover pitifully low levels of piety in various parishes. What is important is that he/she realizes that the Church on earth must continually struggle to incarnate the Kingdom of God, and will always do so imperfectly. With this in mind, the potential convert can guard against a naive or unrealistic approach to the life of the Church.

A convert must also remain aware of the possible temptations within himself that would rob him of the full joy which is the inheritance of an Orthodox Christian. In a convert, there is often a tendency toward fanaticism, a phenomenon observable outside of Orthodoxy as well as within it. Thus, Roman Catholics joke about converts being "more Catholic than the Pope". Those who are deeply committed to and excited about the faith can be led astray into paths of legalism and obsession with external "correctness." Such an attitude, if unhindered, can distract the convert from true concern with living the life in Christ and thus inhibit spiritual fruitfulness.

The glory of the Orthodox Church is that she has preserved the unbroken tradition of life in the Spirit which alone makes authentic Christianity possible. In our age, the Roman Church continues adrift, seemingly unable to find her moorings. Protestantism offers only the stark alternatives of Fundamentalism and Liberalism. The witness of Orthodoxy is therefore all the more crucial to the spiritual condition of humanity. Those of us who have found the presence of the living Christ in her bosom rightfully rejoice in it, yet "our treasure must not be buried in the ground." It is my prayer that we will also take the courage to proclaim Him faithfully to the world.

My Voyage To Orthodoxy

by Father John W. Morris

The sweet smell of incense filled the air. The soft light of candles and hanging lamps flickered in front of the icons on the iconostasis. Above the altar, the Theotokos stretched out her arms in an expression full of love. High in the dome, Christ the Pantocrator looked down on the service in majestic splendor. Towards the front of the chapel, a young man in an ill-fitting, borrowed cassock waited for his turn to kneel before the Archbishop to be made a Reader and to receive his seminarian's cross. He was somewhat uncomfortable and nervous, as many thoughts went through his mind. He had left family and friends in the Southwest to travel halfway across the country to Boston to enter Holy Cross Greek Orthodox School of Theology. He had given up a teaching career, for which he had prepared with eight long years of higher education, to be a student again. He had even left the church of his forefathers to become an Orthodox Christian.

However, as the service went on around the young man, something inside of him told him that he was doing the right thing. After years of searching for the truth about God and Christ, he had finally found it in a small Orthodox Church in Austin, Texas. Although for years, he had resisted the small voice inside of him that had told him since adolescence that he should enter the ministry, he had finally yielded and was about to begin formal preparation for the priesthood. I was that young man and what follows is the story of my spiritual voyage from Protestantism to Orthodox Christianity and from the halls of academia to the priesthood.

I grew up in Oklahoma City, Oklahoma in a Christian family. My parents took me to Sunday School at the local Methodist Church. Although my mother's family were Baptists, my father's family had been active in the Methodist Church for several generations. My grandfather, uncle, and cousins on my

41

father's side had all become Methodist ministers. My parents and grandparents read Bible stories to me as a child and taught me to pray.

I first became interested in religion when my parents sent me to summer camp in Colorado. They did not realize it, but teaching at the 'non-denominational Christian' camp had a strong bias that I now recognize as Calvinistic Baptist. Although I did not know a great deal about the Bible, I doubted their simplistic beliefs. The doctrine of "once saved, always saved" seemed illogical. Despite their arguments, I could not accept the idea that once a person has accepted Christ, his salvation is assured no matter what he does. Logic told me that a person who turns against Christ by refusing to repent of his sins cannot be assured of salvation no matter how sincere or real his initial commitment had been. As a result of this experience I began to study the Bible seriously for the first time. This led to a deeper relationship with Christ, but also confirmed my suspicions that in order to "be saved" a person must strive to live a Christian life. As a result, I became more active in my Church and began to consider entering the ministry.

A few years later, when my parents' marriage ended in divorce, my faith in Christ became my major consolation. I studied the Bible even more, and began attending revivals. I "came forward" several times a year to rededicate my life to Christ. However, the more I read the Bible, the more I doubted the simplistic teaching of Evangelical Protestantism. The more I grew, the shallower my religious life seemed. I needed something more than an emotional experience following the singing of another verse of a hymn and a walk down the aisle to recommit my life to Christ. Indeed, I wondered what followed initial commitment, and I could not find a satisfactory answer from the preachers at the revivals. I grew to realize that as important as acceptance of Christ may be, this is only the beginning of the Christian life. The Bible clearly teaches that only those who strive to live a Christian life will be saved. For Our Lord said, "Not everyone who says to me 'Lord, Lord' shall enter the Kingdom of heaven, but he who does the will of my father who is in heaven." (Matthew 7:21). Indeed, mere belief in Christ is not enough, for as St. James wrote: "You believe that there is one

God. Good! Even the demons believe that and shudder". (Epistle of James 2:19).

At the same time, I found the growing liberalism within the Methodist Church very disturbing. I believed what I read in the Bible. Thus I could not accept the skepticism of the youth leader of my parish or the speakers at youth retreats, who questioned such hallowed doctrines as the Virgin Birth of Christ or His Bodily Resurrection. I recognized and still recognize the importance of science. However, regardless of popular opinion, science is not "truth". Science is only the interpretation by scientists of information that they happen to have at the moment. Whenever they discover new data, these interpretations change.

My later studies of the history of science only reinforced my skepticism of science as the source of all truth. At one time scientists believed that the sun and stars revolved around the earth. Before Copernicus, this was scientific fact. It was scientific fact, but it was wrong, because new data forced the scientists to completely change their theories. Time and again, new information has revolutionized the scientific world and led to the rejection of ideas considered to be facts by previous generations of scientists. If God created the world, God had established the laws of nature, and is powerful enough to cause a virgin to have a child, do miracles, and even to raise Christ from the dead. Science has great value, but should not become a religion. Science can describe the world that God created, and even how it was created, but is too limited and too subject to change to discover the truth about God, who is eternal and changeless.

The "Social Gospel", so fashionable in Methodism during the 1960's, could not fulfill my spiritual needs. Our youth director and many clergy became obsessed with a passion for social justice. As important as these things are, humans cannot create a utopia through their own efforts. The major purpose of the Church is not social activism, but salvation. Later my studies of history only confirmed my adolescent suspicions. Throughout history people have tried to create perfect societies, only to fail because of the shortcomings of human institutions. A study of the 17th and 18th centuries, the "Age of Reason", shows the folly of human efforts to create a utopia through their own endeavors. During this time of the Enlightenment, great thinkers taught that people could create an ideal society through human

43

reason alone. However, despite the influence, this was one of the most violent periods of human history. One war followed another, as the philosopher kings, who spent so much time listening to the prophets of the cult of human reason, fought to enlarge their own realms at the expense of other philosopher kings. It was a time of great thinkers, but also a time of great social injustice and oppression of the lower classes by their upper class patrons. Significantly, this great "Age of Reason" ended in the terror of the French Revolution, during which the heirs to the Enlightenment in France slaughtered thousands in their effort to create a perfect society based on human reason.

More recently, the followers of Karl Marx in Russia and other communist countries have tried to use "scientific socialism" to create a man-made paradise on earth. The result was not equality for all, but rule by bureaucrats in the enslavement of millions under the tyranny of Communism. Thus, I could not accept the arguments of the idealists who rushed to embrace every movement for social justice, because I doubted that humans could ever create a utopia by their own power. The painful reality is that humans are imperfect and cannot create a perfect society based on their own imperfect efforts. I also believed Christ's words, "My kingdom is not of this world". (John 13:36). Thus I believed that the primary purpose of the Church is salvation of souls, not the creation of a perfect society in this world.

At that time, I decided to seek a license to preach in the Methodist Church. As a result, I began a more organized study of the Bible and of Church history. Soon, I discovered that Christianity did not begin with Wesley or even with the Protestant Reformation. I also realized the importance of historic Christianity and Holy Tradition, because I saw one needs guidance to understand the contents of the Bible. There are hundreds of different Protestant sects, all of which claim to present the true teaching of the Holy Scriptures. Thus I realized that one could not understand the Bible through one's own efforts, as the Protestants believe. If anyone could correctly understand the Scriptures, I reasoned, all would interpret it the same way. Instead, Protestantism has produced many different and conflicting interpretations of the Bible, all claiming to be true. I reasoned that God would not leave His people to wander around a spiritual wilderness of conflicting beliefs. Instead, I believed that God revealed the truth to His people and has guided the Church to preserve that truth from one generation to another. As a result, I began to search for beliefs with historical authenticity as a guide to the correct interpretation of the Bible.

Through my studies I began to recognize the importance of the Sacraments. Although Christ said, "Unless you eat the flesh of the Son of Man and drink his blood you have no life in you," (John 6:53), the Methodists had Holy Communion only a few times a year, and then could not tell me what it really meant. I wrote an article in the youth newsletter of my parish based on the Biblical teaching that Holy Communion is a real partaking of the Body and Blood of Christ. The Pastor was horrified and told me very firmly that the bread and grape juice only symbolized the Body and Blood of Christ. Yet Christ said, "This is my body." He did not say, "This symbolizes my body." I asked my Sunday School teacher what Baptism meant and received no satisfactory answer. I also discovered the doctrine of Apostolic Succession. I then realized that the self-proclaimed ministry of the Protestants lacked an essential link to the historic Church. I began to doubt the completeness of the teachings of the Methodist Church.

Therefore at the age of 16, I had grown away from the shallow emotionalism of evangelicalism and had rejected the skepticism of liberalism. I had also begun to believe in Sacraments, Holy Tradition, and a more historical form of worship. As a result, I left the Methodist Church of my fathers and became an Episcopalian. My studies of Wesley had led me to Anglicanism, which I then felt was a branch of the historic Catholic Church. The stately worship of the Episcopal Church, especially the "High" parish that I joined, moved me and fulfilled my religious needs, at least for a time. I mistakenly believed that Anglicanism stands firmly upon the historic Faith as had been taught by the Apostles and their successors and would not change to conform to the latest theological fad.

When I was graduated from high school, I entered Oklahoma City University, intending to prepare myself for Episcopal seminary. During my freshman year, I became a Lay Reader. However, in college I developed a passion for learning, especially the learning of history, that eventually became the major factor in my life. I studied the German language and spent a semester at

Schiller College in Kleiningersheim, Germany. Germany and its history fascinated me. Meanwhile, my professors encouraged me to pursue an academic career. Confused, I went to see my priest, who advised me to develop my talents in history, for I was young and could still study for the priesthood after graduate school. His words were prophetic, "If God wants you to be a priest, you will eventually become a priest." As it turned out, he was right. However, God would first lead me to His Holy Orthodox Church.

In 1970, I entered Oklahoma State University, which had given me a graduate assistantship. Although I continued to attend the Episcopal Church faithfully, I soon adopted the prevailing attitudes of my fellow graduate students. The quest for knowledge and academic excellence became the driving force in my life. After I completed my M. A. a year later, I received a Fulbright Fellowship and spent an exciting year at Goethe University in Frankfurt, Germany. When I returned to complete my Ph.D., I married Cheryl Haun, who was a graduate student in American history.

In 1974, I completed my doctorate and joined the faculty of a small college near Austin, Texas. There, as I drowned in committee work and began to learn of faculty politics, my youthful idealism turned to cynicism. Although many of my colleagues were dedicated teachers and scholars, not all of them shared my total devotion to the quest for knowledge and academic excellence. Instead, the chief interest of some was the preservation of their positions and advancement of their careers. Indeed, some of the older tenured faculty were terrified that the younger, and more enthusiastic, professors would achieve more than they, thereby threatening their positions. Thus, I learned, much to my distress, that academic life is just as shallow as the evangelical Protestantism I had rejected as an adolescent.

At that same time, I accepted a contract to write a history of Nazi Germany. Although I knew something about the subject, the major emphasis of my study of German history had been the 18th and 19th centuries. The intense investigation of this terrible era only sharpened my disillusion with rationalism. Germany had produced Kant, Goethe, and some of the greatest minds of modern history. It was the home of Bach, Beethoven, Mozart, and a score of great composers. Yet this land of cultural greatness had produced one of the most barbaric tyrannies of history. All the intellectual accomplishments of the Germans vanished in the face of the Nazi dictatorship. Indeed, the German students, heirs to the glorious civilization of their forefathers, had rushed to don brown shirts of Hitler's followers. The Nazis even perverted science to produce the philosophy of Aryan racism. The people that had produced modern physics built the gas chambers. This final disenchantment with human reason left me more confused than ever. It convinced me that human knowledge could never provide meaning to my life. I felt like Goethe's Faust who had studied all knowledge and yet finally recognized that he knew nothing of value.

My disenchantment with academic and human reason reawakened the old feeling that I should enter the ministry. I even wrote the Episcopal Bishop of Texas and visited the Episcopal seminary in Austin to investigate a possible vocation. However, at that time I began to question the commitment of Anglicanism to historical Christianity and doctrinal purity. Much to my distress, I learned that there is not one Episcopal Church, but many. The "Low Church" Anglicans of Central Texas rejected many of the "High Church" beliefs and practices that I held dear. My wife and I would often return home from Morning Prayer at the small mission that we attended, wishing that we could worship as we had during our visits to my home parish in Oklahoma. Indeed, there is so much diversity within the Episcopal Church that one may believe almost anything and be a good Episcopalian. One may hold semi-Orthodox beliefs, as I did, or may reject the Virgin Birth of Christ and the Resurrection, as even some Anglican bishops have done. Because I realized that my personal "Catholic" beliefs were outside of the mainstream of American Anglicanism, I decided that I would only be intensely unhappy as an Episcopal priest.

During this time, a climate of doubt and change swept through the entire Episcopal Church which made it impossible for persons really committed to historical "Catholic" Christianity to remain Anglicans unless they completely ignored the real situation in their church. In a few short years, the Episcopal Church cast aside the stately worship that had first attracted me to Anglicanism. Instead, the Episcopalians secularized their services and watered down the doctrinal content of their liturgical texts as they tried one experimental liturgy after another. The Episcopalians, who claimed to be Catholic, rejected almost 2,000 years of Tradition to yield to the pressures of feminism and to ordain women. Bishops and clergy accepted all the liberal ideas that had alienated me from Methodism as an adolescent. Nothing was sacred. No traditional Christian belief escaped questioning, not even the Virgin Birth or the Resurrection. Some Anglicans rationalized justifications for homosexuality, abortion, and immorality of every description as they rushed to embrace the latest fad in theological circles.

Finally, I had to admit to myself what my study of history had already taught me. One of the areas on my Ph.D. had been English history. I had also taught several courses in English history. However, for years, I had ignored what I had learned. Queen Elizabeth I and her advisors had deliberately designed a new religion for her realm that would please as many as possible by adopting weak doctrinal statements that could be interpreted in many different ways. Archbishop Thomas Cranmer, the creator of *The Book Of Common Prayer,* had been a follower of Zwingli, one of the most radical of the Protestant leaders. I had long recognized intellectually that Anglo-Catholicism was far from the mainstream of Anglicanism and was probably only a religious form of English Romanticism. Thus, I finally had to admit to my heart what my mind told me. The Episcopal Church, despite all its claims, is nothing more than a comprehensive form of liturgical Protestantism with very little, if any, commitment to the great teachings of the historic Catholic Church.

At this point, Christ entered my life and led my wife and me to Orthodoxy. One of my minor fields on my Ph.D. had been Russian history. I had also studied Russian language and literature as an undergraduate. Thus, I had developed a great admiration for Orthodoxy. Even as a teenager, Orthodoxy had attracted me. I had attended services at St. Elijah's Orthodox Church in Oklahoma City and read several books on Orthodox Christianity. I had hoped and prayed that the Episcopal Church would unite itself to the Orthodox Church and had joined an association of Anglicans dedicated to Orthodox-Anglican unity. Thus I was very disappointed as the Episcopal Church grew further and further away from unity with the Orthodox Church.

I was overjoyed when my wife and I discovered St. Elias Antiochian Orthodox Church during a weekend visit to nearby Austin. When I taught a course in Russian history, I took my class to the Divine Liturgy at St. Elias to learn something about the religion of the Russian people. That Sunday proved to be one of the most decisive events in my life. I knew how the emissaries of St. Vladimir had felt when they witnessed the Divine Liturgy in Constantinople. Like them, I knew that I had been in the awesome presence of God. There I felt the sense of the sacred that was lacking in the "Low Church" worship of the Episcopal Church that my wife and I attended. My wife, who had gone with us, and I knew that we would be back.

Almost two years later, we moved to Austin, where my wife, who had completed her Ph. D., and I taught at a local community college. While in Austin, I completed writing two books on Nazi Germany, *Revisionist Historians and German War Guilt* and *The Weimar Republic and Nazi Germany*. Although we joined a local parish of the Episcopal Church, the ever-changing Anglican Church could not meet our religious needs. One Sunday, we went to the early service at our new parish. The new forms of worship left us with an empty feeling. After we left the service, I suggested that we go to the Divine Liturgy at St. Elias, recalling how inspired we had been two years previously. Since that memorable day, my interest in Orthodoxy had intensified. I had bought records of Orthodox music, and had read every book on Orthodoxy that I could find. I had even bought several Orthodox service books and had spent hours trying to understand the complex rubrics.

At St. Elias, we found all that had been lacking in our religious life, an overwhelming sense of the presence of God, beautiful worship, and an unwavering devotion to the faith of the ancient Church. As we listened to the inspiring music, smelled the incense, and saw the vestments and icons, we knew that we had been in the presence of the Holy. For about a month, we went to the early service at the Episcopal Church, and then drove across town to St. Elias for the Divine Liturgy. Finally, we decided to go where we were being spiritually fed and to make St. Elias our spiritual home.

From the very beginning, I had no problem accepting the beliefs and practices of the Orthodox Church. Indeed, I will always be grateful to the Episcopal Church for helping me to grow from Protestantism into a more Catholic faith. However, after I actually became Orthodox and studied Orthodox Theology in depth in seminary, I realized that even the "High" Episcopalians hold beliefs that differ substantially from those of the Orthodox Church. Anglo-Catholics approach Christianity from a Western, rationalistic, and legalistic point of view. They follow patterns of thought stemming from Augustine as distilled by Medieval Scholasticism and post-Renaissance Western theology. They know little of the mysticism of the Eastern Church and of the writings of such great Fathers as St. Gregory Palamas. Indeed, in seminary, I learned that the great division in Christianity is not between Catholicism and Protestantism, but between Eastern and Western thought.

Eventually, I had to change my whole approach to the Christian Faith to conform to the less rationalistic mystical theology of the Eastern Church. Although, I had little difficulty making the transition, I have found, especially since I have become a priest, that many converts to Orthodoxy only abandon their "Western" patterns of thought with great difficulty, if at all. Some continue to think in legalistic terms that open their minds to the influence of extremists who claim to represent "true Orthodoxy" and who take great pleasure in judging the leaders of the canonical Orthodox Church. Actually, these "Super Orthodox" exhibit the worst aspects of Western legalism. They confuse The Faith with long beards, the Julian Calendar, and 19th century clerical garb. They fail to realize that strict adherence to the Tradition of the Church does not require a legalistic following of every custom from the past. Others continue to hold to Protestant ideas and cannot totally abandon their past to become completely Orthodox. Instead, they try to pick and choose what aspects of The Faith they will accept. As one of my fellow converts, the Rev. Fr. Gregory Phelan, said at the time that we were receiving instruction, "You have to come to the Church on the Church's terms."

Although, I had no difficulty accepting Orthodox doctrine, a great inner struggle accompanied my conversion to Orthodoxy. Cheryl was ready to join the Church from the very beginning. However, I treasured my British heritage and found it very difficult to give up my idealized view of Anglicanism. Despite my disillusionment, I still hoped that somehow the Episcopal Church would turn away from Protestant liberalism and become Orthodox. I had worshipped in the towering cathedrals of England and admired British history and institutions. I also wondered how an "American" would be accepted in a Church considered foreign by most Americans. However, I soon realized that I had to face reality. Anglicanism was not what I wanted it to be and would never be. Indeed, at this time, the General Convention of the Episcopal Church voted to ordain women, shattering my hopes that the Anglican Church would ever unite with the Orthodox Church. All the loyalty to my ethnic heritage could not save my soul. Indeed, only the true Gospel of Jesus Christ can bring salvation, not ethnicism. Fortunately, St. Elias, as a parish of the Antiochian Archdiocese, worshipped mostly in English. The Pastor, the Rt. Rev. Mark Pemberton, was himself a convert to Orthodoxy. The people of the parish were very friendly and welcomed converts, thus I very quickly overcame my fears of joining a "foreign" Church and decided to follow Christ where I knew that He was leading me, into Orthodoxy.

After several months of instruction, my wife and I received chrismation on Theophany, 1977, with about twenty others, including the present Rev. Fr. Gregory Phelan, Pastor of St. Mary's Orthodox Church in Cambridge, Massachusetts. Tears filled our eyes after we actually became Orthodox Christians. We were so moved after we took Holy Communion that we could not speak. For the first time in our lives, we knew what it meant to be a Christian. Our Orthodox Faith filled the void in our lives and gave us a new direction. Gradually, the old feelings of my youth came back, and I decided to enter the priesthood. After two of the most wonderful years of our lives, we left friends who had become family at St. Elias, a parish that we deeply loved. I cried as I drove past St. Elias for the last time on my way to Boston to Holy Cross, where Metropolitan Philip had sent me to study.

Thus, on September 13, 1978, I waited in the Holy Cross Chapel during Great Vespers of the Feast of the Elevation of the Holy Cross to become a Reader and to begin my seminary education. Two years later, I left Boston, an Orthodox priest. It had been difficult. It was not easy to become a student after having been a professor for several years. There was little money, and we often faced financial hardships. Boston was not Austin, and it was hard to adjust to New England after having lived almost my whole life in the Southwest.

Then in my last year at Holy Cross, Cheryl and I faced the greatest crisis of our lives. Much to our joy after almost eight years of marriage, we were finally going to have a baby. However, our happiness soon turned to agony when we learned that she had caught rubella, German measles, during the crucial period of her pregnancy. The doctors pressured us to have an abortion, terrifying us with stories of mental retardation and physical deformity. However, we refused to murder our child. My studies of the crimes of Nazi Germany had led to a deep respect for human life that included opposition to abortion. Indeed, one of the major reasons we had left the Episcopal Church was its failure to condemn abortion. In our hour of trouble, we turned to Christ. Cheryl received Holy Unction on the Feast of the Annunciation. Later that year, on the Feast of the Dormition, Cheryl gave birth to a normal, healthy, baby boy. Thus Christ saved our child from the rubella. The Theotokos had heard our prayers that she ask her Son to protect our child.

Thus my spiritual voyage has led me to Orthodoxy. Through Orthodoxy, God has given a new meaning to my life, a meaning that far exceeds anything I experienced during my happiest and most idealistic days as a graduate student and college professor. Through Christ's Holy Church, I found historical authenticity, for only the Orthodox Church has preserved the faith of the Fathers and the ancient undivided Catholic Church without change. Christ and His Apostles founded the Orthodox Church, not Henry VIII, Elizabeth I, Wesley, or some other man. No matter where I go in the entire world, the Orthodox Faith will be the same. Orthodoxy has preserved its Faith through persecution by ancient Rome, Islam, the Turks, and contemporary Communism, and will not abandon its Faith to embrace the ever-changing fads of modern liberal theology. Through Orthodox worship and spirituality, I found the real and the powerful sense of the presence of God.

Today many men and women are searching for meaning in their lives. The answer to their quest is Orthodox Christianity. Unfortunately, many find the path to Orthodoxy very difficult. Some even waste their lives in a vain quest for meaning through every possible source but Christ—money, power, fame, pleasure, to name a few. Among those who finally recognize that only Christ can give meaning to their lives, few take the time to seek the historical Christianity through a serious study of the Bible and Church history. Indeed, many are content with a simple faith with little requirements and no sacrifices. Thus they embrace the shallow spirituality of the television preachers and Protestant Evangelicism. Some become trapped in the worship of human reason and change their beliefs according to the latest fad of liberal theology in a vain quest for relevance.

Others refuse to overcome their own ethno-centrism and refuse to consider seriously the case for a religion considered "foreign" by many Americans. Although some actually recognize the truth of Orthodoxy, they cannot liberate themselves from their own ethnic prejudices to embrace Orthodoxy. Indeed some are so devoted to American ethnicism that they refuse to recognize the legitimate need of most Orthodox Churches to use some foreign languages during their worship to minister to the many foreign-born Orthodox Christians in America.

Unfortunately, the Orthodox often contribute to this problem. We fail to witness effectively to the fullness of the truth that we have preserved. Sometimes, we are suspicious of outsiders and fail to welcome potential converts. Sadly, some of us are so ethno-centric ourselves that we seek to transform our churches into societies for the preservation of ethnicity. Some reject any suggestion that we should use enough English to minister to those born in America, not to mention converts. Some see the Church in terms of their own ethnic heritage and refuse to cooperate with Orthodox from a different ethnic heritage, thus perpetuating the unfortunate division of Orthodoxy in this country into ethnic jurisdictions. Orthodoxy is not a society for the preservation of ethnicity. Orthodoxy is the Church founded by Christ to bring all, regardless of ethnic heritage, to the fullness of the truth. If we fail to welcome converts and to minister to their needs, then we fail to obey the command of Christ to preach the Gospel to all nations, including America.

Throughout the years, I will always remember that day at Holy Cross when I became a Reader. On that day, I began a new chapter in my life, a chapter that would lead me to the Holy Priesthood. Although not all are called to become priests, all are called to enter Christ's Holy Orthodox Church. Indeed, all who seek a closer relationship with God should turn to His Church, for it is in His Church, the Orthodox Church, that we enter into the closest relationship with our Creator that is possible in this life. All who have the courage to seek the truth will find fulfillment within Orthodoxy.

My Journey of Faith: A Love Story

By Maria King

Late one Monday afternoon in August of 1978, I was sitting in my living room saying Vespers from the Episcopal Monastic Breviary. My mouth was saying the Psalms but my mind was thinking about what to do.

What had caused me to want to leave the Episcopal Church? Many things: the unwillingness of the national Church to take a stand on moral issues and values, to speak out in favor of life and against abortion, in favor of chastity and against pre-marital, extra-marital, and homosexual sex; to preserve the moral standard of the priesthood. I believed that for a Church to refuse to set standards and guidelines for her own people on the issues that affected them was being unfaithful to the teachings of our Lord and of Holy Scripture. By continuing to be a member of such a body I felt I was in some way condoning those things, even though in my own parish church the moral standards were taught and upheld. The ordination of women to the priesthood was the last straw. I could not accept it as being in accord with the Will of God. Was my opposition to women's ordination the voice of God speaking within or was I being prejudiced? To answer this question I set aside that "still small voice" within and began to explore the matter intellectually. Now, as an Orthodox Christian, I know that when investigating a question one should never set aside and ignore that inner voice.

Under the guidance of a learned priest, several people in my parish church began to study the ordination of women, beginning with an intense two-year study of priesthood, sexuality, and other related topics. During this time we were drawn into a far deeper discovery of mystery than we had ever imagined possible. By "mystery" I mean a sense of the awesome, of religious truths that can be known only by God's revelation and which are so great that they can be known only in part by man's finite mind. We started our study to find the Will of God but encountered mysteries far beyond our comprehension: the mystery of the priesthood, the mystery of the Church, the mystery of the Incarnation of Christ, the mystery of masculinity and femininity with their symbolic meanings and relationships to the priesthood and the Church.

We read and reflected on appropriate passages in the Bible, the writings of the Holy Fathers, the historical texts of the Church, and the books and articles written in the last twenty years in favor of and in opposition to the ordination of women. Most of these were helpful, but reading was not enough. Reflection on what was read, spending time being quiet with God and asking for His viewpoint were and are equally, if not more, important.

In 1976, when the Episcopal Church voted officially to ordain women to the priesthood I knew I had to leave. But where would I go? I had to go to a Church which had Apostolic Succession, where the sacraments were real, true, valid. For me there were only two choices: the Roman Catholic Church, with which I was fairly familiar, and the Orthodox Church, of which I was only slightly knowledgeable. It had become clear to me that Holy Tradition, history, and theology all supported a solely male priesthood. The intuitive response I had felt was the voice of God speaking within me. At last I had an answer to my question. Little did I know at the time that God was whetting my appetite for the WORLD OF MYSTERY that is ORTHODOXY!

My pilgrimage from the Episcopal Church to the Greek Orthodox Church took three years: one year of study, one year to tear myself away from my beloved parish church, and one year as a catechumen. In that first year of study, as I read about the teachings of the Orthodox Church, I knew in my heart where I should be, what I should become. In the depth of my being I sensed the truth of Her teachings and knew that here at last was the fullness of faith—not taken away from, altered, or added to—the 'faith once delivered to the saints': the True Faith!

For two years I had vacillated, because I greatly loved my Parish church of Saint Alban's in Augusta, Georgia. Twelve years before, as a sister, I had conducted the first racially integrated Children's Mission in Augusta, a high powered Vacation Bible School. I had taught many of the adults when they were children. For the last few years the priest had given me the charge of teaching the acolytes* their duties. I loved this work. The young people were beautiful. We spent hours on explanations of the symbolism in the Liturgy, how it touched their personal lives, and the logistics of serving at the altar. They were like my own children. How could I leave them? How could I give up this work?

Yet, how could I stay? After a couple of years God brought a young man back into the parish whom I had trained as an acolyte years before and who worked exceptionally well with young people. He would be a good acolyte master and I knew I could entrust my children to him. This seemed like an indication from God that it was time for me to go. One Monday evening as I was saying Vespers I felt in my heart that Jesus asked me a question. Quietly and gently He asked: "Which do you love more, Saint Alban's or Me?"

"You, Lord, You!"

"If you love Me," He said, "I want you to become Orthodox. You have told me you want to see and know so much. If you become Orthodox, I can show you those things now in this life."

The next day I met with my spiritual father of ten years and told him what had happened and of my decision. He unhappily gave me his approval. That was Tuesday. On Wednesday, I went to see Father Emmanuel, the Greek Orthodox priest in Augusta.

Father Emmanuel was not at all pleased with my decision but did consent to give me instruction. I began attending the Greek Orthodox Church of the Holy Trinity every Sunday.

"Father, I have decided to become Orthodox!"

"Oh, why is that?"

A fleeting look of scepticism fled across his face. There was no smile, no welcome.

"Because it is the True Faith!"

"Why else?"

"Because of the Divine Liturgy. It is so beautiful. When I come here, even though I cannot receive Holy Communion, I feel so close to God, so lifted up that my feet do not touch the ground for three days!"

"Why else?"

---

* Altar boys and girls.

57

"Because the Orthodox Church is not afraid to take moral stands."

"Why else?"

"Because of the music. It carries me to another plane of being closer to God. It is ancient. I feel like we are holding hands with Christians down through the ages and are worshipping God together with them."

"Why else?"

"Because the Divine Liturgy is so mystical. . .so beautiful. The lights, the colors of the vestments, the icons, the incense, the bells, the symbolism in all of the actions during the Liturgy. . .all touch me deeply. It feels so right. . .so good, so of God."

"You have a Church," Father Emmanuel said. "You are active in it. It is better if you take some of the things that we do, our use of icons, some of our prayers, and our way of looking at life back with you to the Episcopal Church. We believe that it is better for someone who is not Greek and who is not marrying a Greek to learn from us and to take the things that appeal to them back to where they are. That way they have the things which they like here to enrich and broaden their own faith. You are Western. We are Eastern. We think differently. It would involve a whole new way of looking at the world. Most people cannot do that, cannot change so completely. You would feel out of place and lonely. It is better that you stay where you are."

"NO! It is NOT better that I stay where I am. This is a BETTER way. It is the TRUE way! I realize it is different but I CHOOSE it! I WANT it!"

"You started off in the Presbyterian Church. Then you became an Episcopalian. Now you want to become Greek Orthodox. What will you want to become next? The Orthodox Church is not something you go through. It is for life. You say you have made a decision. You do not know enough about the Greek Orthodox Church to have made a decision."

The fact was that as a child, though I thought of myself as a Christian, believed in Jesus and that He had died to save me from my sins, I had not been baptized. I said prayers of sorts and read the Bible. My mother and father often spoke of God and His goodness to us. We never ate a meal without first saying grace nor went to sleep without saying our prayers. But though I knew ABOUT God, I did not KNOW Him. Then one night at the age of sixteen, I met Jesus Christ within me, and my whole life was changed, transformed forever. I loved Him with my whole heart and wanted only to be with Him and to please Him, to spend the rest of my life serving Him and bringing others to know Him, that they also might rejoice in Him and His great love. Later, I was baptized in the Presbyterian Church. After seven years, God led me, in my pilgrimage to a fuller expression of the Christian faith, to the Episcopal Church. For twenty-two years I was a most active member of that Church. The first fifteen years were very happy and I was proud to be an Episcopalian. During that time God, in His mercy, permitted me to enter a monastic community and to live as a nun for nine years. For two of those years He graciously allowed me to fulfill my desire to be a foreign missionary. This desire was something He had placed in my heart on the night of my conversion when I gave Him my heart. I loved the monastic life but left it to serve the people of God in a more active way. I was dispensed from my monastic vows in 1968 but continued to serve the parish church in several capacities.

"Father, I have studied for two years! I have a lot more to learn, but I know enough to know this is what I want, and want for the rest of my life."

"Tell me why else you want to be Greek Orthodox?"

"Orthodox, not Greek Orthodox. I'm an American. If there were an O.C.A.[1] church here I'd have gone there. There is not. When an O.C.A. church is formed here I shall go to it. For now, I am here. Being Orthodox is the important thing." (I was soon to change my tune on that.)

"You cannot separate the Greek from the Orthodox." He looked at me with great conviction. "Even if a person does not have Greek blood flowing in his veins, if he is an Orthodox Christian he is also Greek. Greek has to do with the way of thinking and with the Greek spirit. It was through the Greeks that the world was Christianized. . .the Greek language, Greek thought, Greek people."

"I'm sorry, Father I don't see it that way. The Greek part is ethnic, cultural. It is the Orthodox part I desire." (I was soon to eat all of those words!)

---

[1] Orthodox Church in America. One of the several jurisdictions of Orthodox Christians in America, formerly part of the Russian Orthodox Church.

"Why else?"

"Because of the icons. They are very beautiful. Special! They make me quiet inside."

"Why else?"

"Because of the Greek people. They are so beautiful, especially their eyes! I feel that the special beauty in their faces, the light in their eyes and the joyfulness within them comes from their Faith, from receiving Holy Communion since they were babies, and from praying with icons."

"Why else?"

"Because the Orthodox Church will never ordain women to the priesthood."

"Why else?"

"Because, Father, it is the TRUE FAITH! I realize that there is much beauty and truth in the Episcopal Church. I love the Episcopal Church. But in integrity I can no longer stay there." Then I told him the story of my pilgrimage.

I was getting very distressed and even frightened. What would I do if this priest refused me entrance? The questioning had gone on for one hour. I was convinced this was where I should be. The closest Orthodox Church was an hour and a half away, rather inconvenient for frequent visiting! I did not know what else to say to him. "Father, obviously I cannot give you the answer you want," I sighed in exasperation. "All I can tell you is that mine is a response of love!"

Then he smiled! When he smiled I relaxed. Little did I know that the battle was not anywhere near being over. He finally agreed to give me instruction in the Greek Orthodox Faith as long as I understood that this did not guarantee my being chrismated.

On Sundays I went to the Greek Orthodox Church for Orthros* and Divine Liturgy. I was greatly moved, even though I was not permitted to receive Holy Communion. I felt I was in Heaven itself! During the week I continued to go to my parish church and to the convent for Holy Communion because at that time I felt it was important for me to make my communion, even if it meant going to the Episcopal church.

* *Matins.*

Father Emmanuel gave me weekly classes on the Greek Orthodox Faith and Tradition. I also continued to read books by Orthodox writers. For the first four months his unwillingness to allow me to become Orthodox troubled me deeply. He was always kind but the answer was always 'no'. I was not permitted to exercise the talents I had used in the Episcopal Church. He told me to come to the Orthodox Church about once every six weeks and to go to Saint Alban's the rest of the time! This I refused to do. When I asked how I should respond to the Stewardship call I was to receive on a particular Sunday afternoon from Saint Alban's I was told to make my pledge for one year and to keep it! He did not want my gifts, my presence, or my money. This hurt and angered me. Why tolerate this kind of treatment? This led me to reconsider my decision. When I reached it the second time, it was firm: if it took the rest of my life for me to be chrismated, let it be so. The Greek Orthodox Church was where God wanted me to be and where I would stay!

The Greek community, the Greek people, were wonderful to me. They made me feel welcome from the beginning. Their love and support meant a great deal to me then as they continue to do today. Ours is a beautiful community of people!

In January I had to have surgery. That event marked my receiving the sacraments of Holy Confession, Holy Unction, and Holy Communion for the last time in the Episcopal Church. From now on I was going to put all of my eggs in one basket—the Greek Orthodox one! I was very much at peace and willing to wait however long it took.

Father Emmanuel came to visit me on the afternoon of my admission to the hospital. I was very pleased to see him. As we were talking I said, "Father, I do not expect to die, but one never knows when one is put to sleep. Please, Father, if I die I want to die an ORTHODOX Christian." With all my heart I said this, trying to hold back the tears.

He sat with his head bowed for what seemed like an eternity. I felt as if my salvation depended on his answer. How could I die outside the Church? My whole being longed to be Greek Orthodox. Finally he turned and looked at me. "I'll take care of it," he said. My joy knew no bounds! All that mattered to me was to be Greek Orthodox. At last I would be! Little did I know that only if I died would I be chrismated. But, if I lived, I later found out, we'd see!

Thanks be to God, the tumor removed during the surgery turned out to be benign. Even though I was willing to wait for chrismation I could not understand why I was being required to do so. Other people who began instruction after me had already been chrismated. My priest kept telling me "when you are ready, you will know, and I will know." I agreed with him but I also believed that I'd be ready by the next major feast, which I was not! Years later I discovered that it was His Grace, Bishop John of Atlanta, who was responsible for holding me back for a whole year. It took my breath away to realize that years before His Grace became my Spiritual Father his awareness through prayer of what was best for me led him to delay my chrismation. The waiting made all the difference in the level of my commitment. At this time he had never met nor communicated with me! God does work in wondrous ways![2]

At long last my prayers were answered. On the Feast of the Koimisis of the Theotokos, August 15, 1979, I was chrismated in the Greek Orthodox Church and given the name of our beloved and glorious Lady, the Theotokos. My Nonnos named me 'Maria' in Greek. I shall be eternally grateful to him—for the name and for its being in Greek — Μαρία is my true, my Greek Orthodox name!

In preparation for the sacrament of chrismation, I made a very simple long-sleeved, floor-length white dress. (I hope to wear it again, God willing, when I fall asleep in the Lord.) Making the dress was one part of the preparation. Living alone, it was easy to make a retreat and spend time in silence, prayer, and fasting before I was anointed with the Holy Oil which had been blessed by our Ecumenical Patriarch Dimitrios I. All that was lacking in my baptism in the Presbyterian Church was made

[2] My first decision was based on the intellect (finding the True Church, if there was a True Church!), on personal taste for the Greek Orthodox way of celebrating the Divine Liturgy, and, of course, on the word of our Lord when He asked me which I loved more, St. Alban's or Him. My second decision was made in the depth of my heart. As I see it, I had to fight so hard to get into the Greek Orthodox Church, to bang on so many closed and locked doors, that whatever obstacles may be thrown in my way in the future, and many have been already, I know I have dealt with worse during my time as a Catechumen . . . and I know beyond a shadow of a doubt that being a Greek Orthodox Christian and living the Greek Orthodox Faith is God's Will for me.

up in the sacrament of Holy Chrismation. This is the teaching of our Holy Orthodox Church. The desire for Himself that God had placed in my heart on the night of my conversion at the age of sixteen was brought to fulfillment in my chrismation—in the radiance, the splendor, the True Light of Orthodoxy! Like she whose saintly name I now bore, in great joy my heart cried out, "My soul magnifies the Lord and my spirit rejoices in God my Saviour!"

All of my life I have wanted to see Jesus Christ. People told me I could see Him in the beauty of His creation, in the eyes of other people, and veiled in the sacrament of His Body and Blood. This was not enough. I still longed to see Him in His Resurrected Body. When He led me into the Greek Orthodox Church and showed me icons. . .that was an answer to prayer and one of the many things I feel sure He meant when He had earlier told me there were things He could show me now in this life if I became Orthodox.

According to the Seventh Ecumenical Council of Nicea (787 A.D.), "The honor paid to the icon passes on to that which the icon represents, and he who reveres the icon reveres in it the person who is represented." In part this means that when we kiss the icon of our Lord and Saviour Jesus Christ or of the Theotokos or any of the Saints, He, she, or they, receive our kiss! We do not know how this happens. It is a mystery beyond our understanding. Icons are far more than beautiful paintings or mosaics that inspire and teach us. In a sense, they are also windows into heaven. Through the eyes of the person portrayed in the holy icon we are able to look into the very eyes of that person, and—wonder of wonders!—that Holy One looks into our eyes and our hearts. If we are quiet and stand there for a while and listen, our Lord or whoever that Holy One is into whose eyes we look may speak to us in our hearts.

Saint John of Damascus writes:

All images reveal and make perceptible those things which are hidden. For example, man does not have immediate knowledge of invisible things, since the soul is veiled by the body. Nor can man have immediate knowledge of things which are distant from each other or separated by place, because he himself is circumscribed by place and time. Therefore, images are a source of profit, help, and salvation for all, since they make things so obviously manifest, enabling us to perceive hidden things. Thus, we are encouraged to desire and imitate what is good and to shun and hate what is evil.

As a catechumen I began praying with an icon of our Lord at eye level at the iconostasion in my room. My priest instructed me to pray for fifteen minutes in the morning and fifteen minutes in the evening, standing in front of my icon, pouring myself into it and looking into the eyes of our Lord while saying the Jesus Prayer: "Lord Jesus Christ, Son of God, have mercy on me, a sinner."

The first time I stood there trying to "pour myself into the icon", saying the Jesus Prayer and looking into the eyes of our Lord, something unexpected happened. The face of Christ began to change and to become other faces before my eyes, while the colors in the icon began to intensify and then return to normal! I had never prayed before an icon before and no one had told me of anything like this.

What was happening? Was this of God or was it of Satan? Not knowing, I began to do what one does to protect himself when he is in the presence of evil: to call on the name of Jesus (which I had been doing all along in saying the Jesus Prayer) and to make the sign of the cross over and over again. I was so frightened by these occurrences that I walked away from the icon.

"Do you not believe that the Lord Who made heaven and earth and holds them all in being cannot cause paint on a piece of wood to move around and light to come out of it?" Father Emmanuel asked the next day. "You do not have enough faith. Go back. The next time it happens, pray 'Lord, I believe. Help my unbelief.' " I took the advice of this holy priest. What Saint Isaac the Syrian said is certainly true: "Thirst after Jesus and He will satisfy you with His love." And Theophan the Recluse: "You seek the Lord? Seek, but only within yourself. He is not far from anyone. The Lord is near all those who truly call on Him. Find a place in your heart and speak there with the Lord. It is the Lord's reception room. Everyone who meets the Lord meets Him there. He has fixed no other place for meeting souls."

The Divine Liturgies of Saint John Chrysostom, Saint Basil the Great, and Saint Iakovos are very beautiful, leading us from our Lord's Nativity to the beginning of His Ministry, to His entry into Jerusalem on that first Palm Sunday and His climbing the Hill of Calvary (both these events being represented in the symbolism of the Great Entrance), to His Crucifixion, Resurrection, Ascension into Heaven, and his Session (being seated) at the right hand of the Father. We feed on the Holy Body and Precious Blood of our Lord and Saviour Jesus Christ at Communion and are nourished with Him. We feed on God Himself!

When I am at the Divine Liturgy I feel like I am no longer on this earth, but in heaven. Although I cannot see or hear them, I sense the presence of our Lord and His Mother, Saint John Chrysostom, Saint Photios the Great and the other saints, the angels and archangels, and hear the music of the Heavenly courts. Could it be that during the Divine Liturgy the Kingdom of God within all of us is perceived more clearly?

It is impossible for me to explain what the Divine Liturgy and receiving Holy Communion mean to me. Everything I do or think or say becomes either a preparation for or an impediment to receiving Holy Communion. I must forgive the people who anger or upset me, because wanting to lash out or get even places me in a state of sin where I cannot possibly receive Holy Communion. Which is more important: doing what I want to do to that person or receiving Jesus Christ? Do I love the sin more than I love Him? There is no alternative but to forgive. Besides, forgiving the person will please Jesus. Saint John Chrysostom writes:

> "It is necessary to know the miracle of the Holy Mysteries—what it consists of, for what purpose it was given, and what profit it brings. 'There is one body', it is said 'for we are members of his body, of his flesh, and of his bones'. (Ephesians 4:4; 5:30) Let the initiated hearken to these words! Thus, in order to be members of the body of Christ not only in love but in actual fact, let us unite with this body. This is done through the food which Christ gave us as a token of His great love for us. For this purpose He joined Himself with us and merged His body with us, so that we should form one with Him, as body and head are joined into one. This is the sign of the greatest love. . ."*

The divine John of Damascus says in *On The Orthodox Faith*, Vol. IV, Chapter 13: "Since we are dual and twofold, our birth must be twofold and our food complex . . . not because the body which ascended to Heaven itself comes down, but

---

* *Discourse on John, 46.*

because bread and wine become transformed into the body and blood of our Lord God. If you wish to know how this happens, it is enough for you to hear: by the Holy Spirit, just as the Lord made His own body by the Holy Spirit from the Holy Virgin for Himself and in Himself. We know nothing more, except that the word of God is true, effective and all-powerful. Of the means we can know nothing."

Saint John of the Ladder says: "If a body coming into contact with another body undergoes a change under its influence, how can a man not change if he touches the body of God with pure hands?" (Chapter 28). It is also written in the Hierondic: "John of Vostros, a holy man who possessed power over impure spirits, asked the demons who lived raging in some possessed maidens saying: 'What are the things you fear in Christians?' They answered: 'Truly you possess three great things: the first is what you wear round your neck; the second is what you wash with in Church; the third is what you partake of in community.' Thereupon he asked them: 'Of these three, which do you fear most?' They answered: 'If you guarded well that of which you partake, none of us could ever offend a Christian.' These things which our deadly enemies fear most are: the cross, baptism, and communion."[3]

I heard Byzantine music for the first time many years before my conversion, when I was a nun stationed at the convent in Augusta, Georgia. When the Eastern and Western Pascha or Easter was celebrated on different dates I used to go to the Good Friday evening Service of the Lamentations. It was all new to me. I was fascinated by everything: the powerful, magnificent Byzantine music, the Greek language, the sound of the bells on the censer, the sweet fragrance of the incense, the warmth of the colors and the lights. . .everything. I had been taught as a Western Christian that it was very important to understand everything that was said, but I had no desire to understand the meaning of the words. It was more than enough to give myself to them, to be caught up in the beauty and glory of this marvelous Byzantine worship!

[3] These quotations were all taken from the chapter on Directions to Hesychasts in the *Writings From the Philokalia on the Prayer of the Heart*, pages 260-264.

In my religious pilgrimage I have been involved with many different forms of religious music, from that in the hymnals of several denominations to folk music used in Folk Masses, to the calm and peaceful Plainsong chanted in monastic houses in the West. In all of these I have enjoyed praising God and have on occasion been deeply touched by the music. But no music ever achieved in me the level of awareness and contemplation of God as that of the ancient Byzantine Liturgical hymns!

What makes Byzantine music so conducive to prayer and meditation, to being still and adoring God? There are several reasons. This magnificent music is sung in beautiful Liturgical Greek in the services of the Greek Orthodox Church. This music was given to us, approved for us, centuries ago by the Fathers of the Church, as were the prayers we pray in church, the form of the services, and the vestments: chosen for us by the Fathers under the guidance of the Holy Spirit. The Byzantine tones are filled ONLY with those qualities that lead us to contrition and to holiness. They move us to a level of being that better enables us to pray, to reflect on our lives, to repent of those things that keep us from giving ourselves completely to God. It is easier in the presence of that holy music to "Be still and know that I am God." (Psalm 46:10)

As there is something mystical about the Byzantine music, so there is something mystical about the Liturgical Greek language. It distresses me to hear that many of our faithful want to change to an entirely English liturgy. The reasons they give are to increase our understanding, to make our people more devout, and, very importantly, to keep the young people in our Church. All highly desirable objectives. Will changing the language accomplish them? Having been through a language change in the Episcopal Church and having had friends who went through one in the Roman Catholic Church, I do not believe English is the solution, for it is not the Greek language that is the problem. Understanding the Liturgy comes not only with study, not only with prayer, but with changing our lives. Many people know English liturgies by heart yet do not understand what they are all about. Their knowledge is of the lips. No particular language will keep our young people in Church! Young people leave Church where only English is spoken. Our youth are quick to perceive the depth of the personal commitment of the people they love to

Christ and His Church, or the lack of depth. I believe that what will keep the young people in Church is their seeing and feeling in their hearts a deep personal commitment on the part of their parents, older brothers and sisters, koumbari, etc., to Our Lord and His Holy Church, that is, of seeing the Orthodox Faith being LIVED by the people that matter to them.

Twenty years ago the Roman Catholic Church used Latin in the Mass. The Episcopal Church used the very beautiful and exalted Elizabethan English of the 1928 Prayer Book. Today, twenty years later, 40% of the Catholic faithful, 21 million Catholics, many of them young, are demanding the option of the Latin Mass. When the Episcopal Church forbade the use of the 1928 Prayer Book in favor of an updated modern English version, many of her faithful were very distressed. Some of them broke away in order to preserve the language, that is, the mystical quality of the worship. Many Episcopalians still speak with longing of the more beautiful English with which they worshipped God years ago. The trauma that both Churches went through was tremendous. And for what? Today, twenty years later, things are not as wonderful as the advocates of the language changes promised. Changing the language increased significantly neither the knowledge nor the devotion of the people, nor did it keep their young people in Church. Perhaps we can learn from their experience.

What is so great about the Liturgical Greek language? Many things. It is the majestic language of the Holy Fathers of the Church. What a privilege to be able to praise God in the very same words and music of Saint John Chrysostom, Saint Gregory the Theologian, Saint Photios the Great, and all the saints! When we sing these hymns we not only praise God but, in a mystical way, we join our voices with that magnificent throng of holy men and women and children who have gone before us!

Greek is the language in which the New Testament is written, the language in which most of the documents of the Ecumenical Councils were written, the language of most of the Holy Fathers of the Church. It is the language in which the great hymnology of the Orthodox Church was written. For these and other reasons it is the mother language of Orthodoxy—be it Greek, Russian, American, Albanian, Serbian, or other. Greek is also the mother language of Christianity for the same reasons, since through the Greek language and the Greek Fathers and Mothers of the Church the World was Christianized.

And one last reason — it is very beautiful![4]

The Greek language of our Liturgies is not a matter of ethnicity or of nationality but of the Orthodox Christian Tradition. It would be ethnic, if the Liturgies were written in Modern Greek. The magnificent Greek of the Liturgies is one of the rich treasures given into our hands for promulgation and safe keeping, as well as for enriching our Faith and our lives.

When I first came to the Greek Orthodox Church I did not know one word of Greek. In the few years I have been in the Church I have studied Liturgical and Biblical Greek. Not having a facility for language, I still have a long way to go! I love the language and find it very vibrant and alive. So much so that I prefer to pray in Greek, and from memory, as books can be a hindrance. Committing these Greek prayers to heart seems to do that literally: they go into and become a part of my heart. Being primarily English speaking, I also pray in English. Some prayers, like the prayer of Saint Ephraim the Syrian, I pray three times: first in Greek, then English, then Greek. That way the prayer is committed to the heart in English, also. Still, my prayers are more deep in Greek. It is a mystery! St. Irenaeus said: "To sing is to pray twice." For me, to pray in Greek is to pray thrice!

My favorite prayer by far is the Jesus Prayer, the prayer of the heart, a wonderful way to pray without ceasing every minute of the day and night. One begins saying it orally, then mentally, then with the heart. The prayer is not magical. It is not enough simply to repeat the words. One must try to live his life as he is taught through the prayer. The Jesus Prayer is many things. Great saints have written about it. It is well to read their works. The *Philokalia* and *The Way of the Pilgrim* teach us much about it.

One way to think of the Jesus Prayer is: we look at Him for whom the prayer is named: "LORD," master of all creation, visible and invisible. "JESUS," Messiah, the one who is coming to save the faithful people. "CHRIST," anointed one. "SON OF

---

[4] In my own parish church, when non-Greek-speaking people are present, our priest celebrates the Divine Liturgy in Greek and English. A person attending two consecutive liturgies will hear the entire service in the language of his choice. This way both groups can show love and compassion for each other and give a little. It works well for us.

GOD," indeed, He is the One begotten of the Father before all ages Who became incarnate in the womb of the Virgin Mary, born for us, lived and suffered and died for us, and rose again that we might have life and have it in all its fullness. "God became man that man might become God", we are told by St. Athanasios. What else can we say in the presence of One so holy and beautiful and pure but "HAVE MERCY ON ME, A SINNER"? This prayer is a great aid to Theosis.[5]

A word about the importance of regular and disciplined Bible reading and study of the Holy Scriptures, the writings of the Church Fathers, and other books on our Holy Faith and Tradition. If we are serious about our life in God, it is imperative that we make time regularly during the day, or at least during the week, for study that is combined with prayer. Study by itself frequently leads to pride and pride always separates us from God. For those who are interested in studying about our Faith, the source par excellence is in the hymns and prayers of the liturgical services of our Church. There is so much to learn about our Holy Faith and Tradition! A life-time is not enough!

Now let's talk about fasting—not fasting for the sake of fasting but fasting for the sake of being obedient to God and His Holy Church, fasting that assists us in our pilgrimage to Theosis. So many of our people think of fasting as an unpleasant thing that one must go through to receive Holy Communion, as an extremely difficult time to be endured, or as an unnecessary and ridiculous exercise. But if fasting begins with the eye and the heart on Jesus, if it is done out of love for Him and out of the desire to have our hardened hearts softened, if it is done to purify our souls and bodies. . .then it is a joy! Fasting must be intimately joined and intertwined with prayer, preferably prayer that is without ceasing. Whether it is the Jesus Prayer or another brief prayer repeated over and over for a constant remembrance of God, it is necessary to pray in order for the fasting from food to be of any value spiritually. It has been my experience that meat and bloody fish, dairy products and (except on Saturdays and

---

[5] Theosis: "deification." As Timothy Ware states in *The Orthodox Church,* p. 29: "If man is to share in God's glory, the Greek Fathers argued, "if he is to be 'perfectly one' with God, this means in effect that man must be 'deified': he is called to become by grace what God is by nature. Accordingly Saint Athanasius summed up the purpose of the Incarnation by saying: "God became man that we might be made god" p. 29. The Greek word is definitive: It means 'becoming god.'

Sundays) olive oil and wine are the easiest things from which to fast. It is the fasting from sin—from being critical of other people, from a tongue that speaks idly and vainly, from trying to get my own way, from clinging to worldly activities—THAT is what is difficult.

When fasting one is both joyful, because one's spirit is light and, at the same time grieving, in a state of penitence. Yet the benefits of fasting—the softening of our hearts, the total dependence on God, the love that grows within us as we hunger for Him, as we strive to please Him in being obedient -- are all worth it! Lenten times are my favorite times of the year. I fast because I want to be free. I fast because I love God and want to please Him. It is very simple and our Lord makes light what seems to others as a heavy burden.

According to Saint John Chrysostom:

> The honor of fasting consists not in abstinence from food, but in abstinence from sinful practices. Do you fast? Give me proof of it. If you see a poor man, take pity on him. If you see an enemy, be reconciled with him. If you see a friend gaining in honor, envy him not. Let not the mouth only fast, but also the eye, the ear, and the feet, and the hands, and all the members of our bodies. Let the hands fast by being pure from avarice. Let the feet fast by ceasing to run to lewd spectacles. Let the ear fast by not listening to false reports. Let the mouth fast by not speaking evil of others. For what doth it profit if we abstain from birds and fishes and yet bite and devour our brethren? The evil speaker eats the flesh of his brother and bites the body of his neighbor.

Fasting times are times of battle with Satan and his army of demons. When we fall into sin, immediate repentence, immediately asking our Lord for His forgiveness and asking the person we have offended for his forgiveness is the action that should be taken. In so doing we win a victory for God and grow in humility, that basic and first virtue without which we shall never reach Theosis.

It is very important to have a Spiritual Father for guidance during these especially difficult times. The important thing in fasting is obedience. Should our Spiritual Father tell us not to fast or to fast only in certain ways, our joyful obedience is more pleasing to God than a strict keeping of the Fast.

Our Holy Church is very compassionate towards her children. Those who are very young, those who are ill or convalescing, those who are very old, are not expected to fast com-

71

pletely. Obedience is the important thing. Submitting our wills to the Will of God is what matters. There are other forms the fasting discipline can take in such cases. It was one of the many discoveries that caused me joy in the Orthodox Church to realize that the fasting periods before Christmas, Pascha, the feast of Saints Peter and Paul, and of the Koimisis of the Theotokos*, are OPPORTUNITIES our Holy Church offers her children. In other Christian Churches where fasting is required, or has been required in the past, with the exception of the very young, the infirm, and the elderly, it was considered a sin not to fast on Fridays and during the Lenten season. In the Orthodox Church there is no such emphasis on sin. Some choose to fast. Some choose not to fast. "God loves a cheerful giver." If our people only realized the inexpressible sweetness and abundant joy they were missing in not taking advantage of living the Lenten times as our Holy Church directs, they would eagerly seek to keep the Fast and to partake of her choice fruits!

One of the things I have found most difficult in becoming fully Orthodox in all my being is the great difference in thinking between the Orthodox and the Western mind. Father Emmanuel did well to warn me of this difference when I first announced my intention to become Orthodox. For the Western, the Heterodox, mind the great thing is understanding. Everything needs to be defined clearly, explained thoroughly, understood, and proven. Things which cannot have this done to them are considered questionable. Effect and cause need to be clear. There are many areas of life in which this type of thinking is desirable, even necessary.

In theology and religion this attitude poses obvious problems. Matters of faith cannot be proven. That is why they are matters of faith! Explaining exactly how the bread and wine become the Body and Blood of Christ is one of the most flagrant examples of the pridefulness and presumption of this way of thinking in the theological area. It is also a legalistic way of thinking, involving strict, literal conformity to the law or religious code. Legalism truly has no place in Orthodoxy.

In the Orthodox way of thinking it is not reason or understanding that is paramount. It is feeling and experiencing. God is

---

* *June 29 and August 15, respectively.*

not a thing to be known about nor a concept to be understood. He is a Person to be loved and experienced. It is this type of approach we need to take in all of our theological and religious life, as we try to live our Faith and grow in holiness. We cannot bind God, nor can we force Him to guarantee our holiness just because we keep the so-called rules of the Faith. Our growth in holiness is His gift, not our due. Often I find myself unconsciously thinking as a Westerner. For those of us living in America this mentality is constantly assailing us through the media and our non-Orthodox friends. It is difficult to "change the mind", that is to "convert", in this area. My experience is that the Orthodox way of thinking is the better way.

Discovery of the Orthodox Faith is wonderful, but discovery is not enough. It is in the response of love for God and for His people, in the day-by-day living of the Orthodox Faith, in being fed with the Body and Blood of Christ, in prayer and good works, in humility and obedience, in imitation of our Lord Himself and of the Theotokos and the other saints through the ages that we who discover this glorious Faith—whether we be already Orthodox Christians at the time or not—may, by the grace of God, reach Theosis.

God has been very gracious to me over the years. Of all the blessings He has bestowed upon me there are three that stand out far above all the others. In essence these three are one: His bringing me to Himself when I was sixteen, His bringing me into the Greek Orthodox Church, and, in time, His bringing me to a wise and holy Spiritual Father. I say these three are one because my Chrismation was the beginning of the fulfillment of my conversion. Through the prayers of my Spiritual Father and through his divinely inspired direction and guidance our Lord and Saviour Jesus Christ will one day bring to fruition that desire and longing He placed in my heart at sixteen: to please Him always and to become all that He wants me to become. In Orthodoxy we call this Theosis.

May God grant the day to come that all men and women and children everywhere may come into the brilliant splendor of the Orthodox Faith, into the fullness of Light, of Faith, of Holiness. . .that altogether we may sing the joyful hymn in the Divine Liturgy of Saint John Chrysostom:

73

We have seen the true light, we have received the heavenly Spirit; we have found the true faith, we worship the undivided Trinity; the Trinity has saved us. Amen.

One + One = One In Christ:
A Conversion Pilgrimage

By Father Gregory Wingenbach

For one in this equation, my wife Mary Ann (Pearce) Wingenbach, the journey began in a southern city and family, mellowed by Dixie's traditions of gentility, politics, horses, and good food and drink. Her home was of mixed religious affiliations, although of basic American ethnic stock. The initial seeds for her questing faith were sown in a Roman Catholic girls' convent school.

For me, Father Gregory Charles Wingenbach—the other side of the equation—home and family were diverse both in religious and ethnic heritages, and the story began in the Nation's Capital.

For both of us, the path would take many varied twists and turns before being resolved within the Orthodox Catholic Church, and more precisely in the jurisdiction of the Greek Orthodox Archdiocese. This is why we tend to disbelieve that— even in the case of Saul's famous conversion into Paul, Saint and Apostle—an authentic conversion is ever the unforeseen, abrupt turnabout in life which pop evangelism and religion's critics portray it as. It's usually "a long time coming."

" From our experience, 'overnight' conversion is how insecure fanatics, looking for the pot at the end of the rainbow, are formed,'' my wife once told a group of priests and presvyteres. "Can a true spiritual rebirth ever take place, without first a time of seeking and finding, or in other words, mature growth and solid development? I doubt it."

True enough, our conversion, this coming to Orthodox faith has been a radical change. Certainly, nothing in our lives can ever be the same, especially given the process and path our conversion experience took.

We can now look back and perceive God's hand in it all. We can even see some elements of a common thread in our very different lives. Still, it's incredible, no matter how we look at it backwards or forwards.

Mary Ann's family, for example, is about as far as you can get from any historical or ethnic connections with traditional Eastern Orthodoxy. They are the descendants of White Anglo-Saxon Protestant and Roman Catholic American pioneers. The common denominator on both sides of her family tree are George Rogers Clark and his brother Jonathan, heroes of the opening to the West and of the American colonists' revolution against England.

As for me, my background and personal odyssey are no less tangled, although my eventual seminary training and leanings make it a bit more plausible, even perhaps somewhat logical by comparison.

I was born the first son in two marriages of an already elderly veteran of the Spanish-American War and of a widow left with five girls to raise at the deepest part of the Depression years. My father Charles, of German-Slavic ancestry, was a Roman Catholic, while my mother Pearl (Stanton) converted after World War I from the Methodist Episcopal tradition to Roman Catholicism.

It was a time when nativist American feelings were once again beginning to run high. The day I was born, the headlines in Washington's newspapers reported a new Nazi conspiracy launched by Adolf Hitler against the fragile, doomed Austrian republic. A German-Jewish nurse, distraught by the growing threat of Nazi Germany, handed the newborn Charles Edward Wingenbach over to my mother with the bitter comment, "Well lady, here's your little Hitler!" My mother never forgot that.

As it turned out, neither my future wife Mary Ann Pearce nor I were destined to escape nativist prejudice. In one form or another, it would be an experience to "dog" our steps in life. When my family moved, in the final months of World War II, from the Nation's Capital to rural northern Florida, even my elderly father—with a lifetime of over 70 years already "under his belt"—was surprised by the latent and outright prejudice that we encountered at times. World War II may have been fought overseas to rid the world of ethnic hatreds and the blight of racism, but at least another generation and more would have to pass before the American homeland would begin to shed some of

76

the old religious and racial prejudices. To many rural residents, people coming from "the North" with unfamiliar accents, folkways, and foreign-sounding names were, at best, "Yankees". Those not of Protestant persuasion, especially Roman Catholics, were tainted by the suspicion of "Papism", particularly in the eyes of fundamentalist, "hard-shell" preachers. Southern public schools were, more often than not, partial extensions of the 'American' (that is, Protestant) religion. Not-so-subtle pressures were exerted at different times in the schools and social life to convert or even drive out those "not like us".

My wife's family had similar experiences as they moved from urban Louisville, Kentucky to rural Indiana and then to southwestern Kentucky. In self-defense of their own ways, Roman Catholic pioneers, who had fled persecution in their native England, had to migrate at least twice in order to enjoy basic social rights. Although they had founded the original colony of Maryland, the Anglo-Irish Catholics had to flee once again, this time to the Kentucky bluegrass country, where they established a foothold which persists to this day. "WASP" prejudice in public institutions forced them to set up their own parochial, or parish-based schools. Even though Mary Ann and her family were descendants of the American Revolutionary and Confederate heroes, they encountered the underlying prejudice of nativist Protestants in a variety of ways.

From her childhood in southwestern Kentucky, Mary Ann recalls that the well-known nativist anti-Catholicism occasionally worked the other way. Deep in that Protestant heartland, an immigrant blue-blood Italian missionary set out with pastoral zeal to "return the Protestants to their Mother Church." And, despite a thick accent and broken English, the diminuitive Father Luigi's pastoral zeal actually did succeed in converting an entire Scots-Irish Presbyterian congregation back to Rome's allegiance!

Regardless, the times were a-changing. Questions were beginning to be asked on both sides that had never occurred to rock-ribbed Protestants or Roman Catholics. America's pluralistic society was bearing its own peculiar fruit. All different kinds and persuasions of people in America were now "bumping elbows" regularly in the marketplace and elsewhere in public life, if not yet in their churches.

77

Mary Ann went off to a girls' convent school, run and taught by nuns. She remembers a high school class in church history, when the East/West schism was being reviewed, albeit ever so briefly. Sister Alberta mentioned that, despite the "schismatics" breakaway from the unity of the Holy Catholic Church of Rome, their ministry of the Sacraments and their Priestly orders have remained valid and intact in Apostolic succession." In fact, the elderly German-American nun pointed out, "if you're ever in a place where there is an Eastern Orthodox church and no Catholic church, you may fulfill your Sunday obligation by attending their Mass."

This was heady stuff and more than a little perplexing for a young girl, conditioned by the uncompromisingly Roman Catholic lectures she'd heard previously from the nuns and at the feet of her cousin, a prominent monsignor who headed the archdiocesan school board. "But, Sister," she asked innocently, "if the Catholic Church and the Pope alone are true successors of Christ and His Apostles, then how can a group which we say has cut itself off from the one true Church still be able to administer the sacraments that Jesus gave to His Church? How can that be possible?"

"Mary Ann", the kindly nun answered, "I've sometimes asked myself that same question. But I know that's what the Holy Father teaches. I guess the only answer is that God handles things in His own providence, no matter what our problems as human beings are."

The incident was brief and soon forgotten. Nevertheless, the question was filed away until a later time of seeking would reawaken it. In fact, it would later be joined by a similar question that I myself was asking as a young Roman Catholic seminarian.

During my boyhood, after our move to Florida, my principal spiritual guide turned out to be an Episcopalian priest of Anglo-Catholic devotion and persuasion. When isolation and family problems threatened and the need for a stable religious and social environment was evident, after a series of disasters had impoverished our family, the Very Reverend Fred Yerkes offered his hand in friendship to us and took my brother Joe and me under his wing. Father Yerkes, as he was popularly called even in fundamentalist northern Florida, saw such needs in quite a few of the boys in the surrounding towns. His response was, for the times, a bold and unprecedented one: he founded a Boy Scout troop which was open to youths of the area, regardless of religious affiliation, under the aegis of tiny Trinity Episcopal Church. The frail Episcopalian vicar nonetheless carefully avoided proselytism; he made every effort to consult with the pastors—Protestant and Roman Catholic—of all the boys involved. He set two requirements in order to maintain a solid religious base for the activities: all of the young scouts were expected to attend regularly and to participate in the boys' choir, church socials, and camping projects alike.

Father Yerkes was, and no doubt still is, a one-man ecumenical experience for those around him. Certainly he was that for us boys, our parents, and the communities we lived in. During a time when it was by no means fashionable, he gave us a role model: that of a concerned, unprejudiced pastor who cared about the Lord's people no matter what church they identified with. If they were in need, he offered his help with no strings attached.

In fact, my very first, embryonic stirrings of curiosity about Orthodoxy came from a couple of offhand conversations that popped up in the course of sessions following our scout meetings. Somebody asked what other kinds of Christians there were. I remember that he turned to the few of us who were Roman Catholic and Episcopalian and observed, "They may say all roads lead to Rome, but it's also true that most roads come *from* the East. It was the early Christian Fathers of the Eastern Churches who first took up where the Apostles left off. Yet, in our self-conceit, few people in the West and especially our American churches care about or even realize that!"

He liked to challenge us, even if we were just pre-teens and teenage country boys whose principal thoughts were work and fun, family and school. Along with two kindly Irish Roman Catholic priests whom my brother Joe and I served as altar boys in what were then tiny mission parishes, Father Yerkes probably helped to influence me more than anyone else to enter the preparatory seminary and study for the priesthood. Early on, when I was "down in the dumps" one day, he took me aside and counseled me, "Charlie, God is calling you to something special. Don't you ever shut your ears to Him, even when you can't see where He's leading you."

79

Not long afterwards, I left Florida and took up the intensive residential program of academic and spiritual formation which was typical of the pre-Vatican II Roman Catholic Church's training of prospective priests. Under the sponsorship of the Bishop of the St. Augustine, Florida diocese, and with the twin recommendations of my Roman Catholic parish priest and the Episcopalian vicar who had always been my spiritual mentor, I entered a minor seminary-college located in the suburbs of Baltimore, Maryland.

The seminary program was akin to that of many private, church-sponsored academies: a solid emphasis on the humanities, a firm grounding in Latin and the classics of Western literature, a modern foreign language, and a fairly strict regimen of orderly discipline. The difference came in the intensive religious instruction and liturgical life, centered around the dawn-to-dusk semi-monastic schedule of chapel services, devotions, and religious counseling.

If there was anything at all "off the mark" or inadequate in what we experienced as seminarians, it would have been the general inability at the time of the seminary Fathers to recognize that we—their 'clientele'—were more or less typical teenage boys. We were immature, away from home, trying to deal with all kinds of emotional and intellectual stirrings in our make-up as young males. We carried a sort of cloister around with us at all times: we were taught to discipline ourselves against the temptations of the world, to exercise a certain degree of "modesty of the eyes," and above all to be wary of feminine companionship which could draw us away from the celibate ideal of the Roman Catholic priesthood. Recreation times, off-campus and during our Christmas and summer holidays, were the occasions of greatest temptation, we were admonished.

Yet, unlike several Roman Catholic priests of the post-Vatican II era who have written commentaries on those days, I'd have to say that my memories of most of our seminary faculty and counselors, as well as of the life we led, were favorable and wholesome. Those men were mostly caring persons who were devoted to the thorough education and moulding of a bunch of youthful unknown quantities, in order to prepare us as best as they knew how for the Roman Catholic priesthood and parochial communities of that day and age. Today, however, even for fairly traditional Roman Catholics, that is a whole world and era away!

In the second year of seminary, I was assigned as a part-time aide to the school librarian. It gave me a readymade opportunity to independently research my favorite interests: history, public affairs, and literature. For a young man destined for the relatively unquestioning standards of the Roman Catholic priesthood, it was not, however, a fortuitous development. I wound up spending a lot of time in the stacks, a section of the seminary library that housed histories of the origins of the Christian Church, the works of the early Church Fathers of East and West, commentaries on diverse Christian liturgies and traditions, and even writings by Eastern Orthodox, Anglo-Catholic, and other non-Roman spokesmen. Not only that: the risque writings of Boccaccio and others of a suggestive nature which were prominent on the Vatican's list of forbidden books occasionally whiled away my off-duty hours.

These exposures rekindled a lively curiosity towards the rest of the world. Leisure-time excursions into nearby Baltimore and Washington D.C. included occasional visits to Orthodox and various "High Church" Episcopalian and Lutheran churches, as well as the "forbidden fruit" of a clandestine date once in a while with a local young girl or two. Such adventures, I recall, were the occasion for more than a dozen of the young seminarians abruptly deciding to quit the institution's cloistered life.

Naturally, I was affected by all of this. Not as drawn into the standardized rhythm of Roman Catholic life, partly because of my very ecumenical upbringing, I was more inclined to delve deeply into fields which some of my professors and peers regarded irrelevant to, or even harmful for, a neophyte seminarian. Increasingly I experienced serious questions about the standard teachings of Roman Catholicism. At least three of the seminary faculty, however, felt it better to encourage inquisitive and searching young minds; their judgment was that the Church would be the better for it in the long run. Foremost among these was the erudite professor of history, who fielded more and more frequently the questions I put to him, in and out of class.

"Father, if the Church began in Jerusalem, the Middle East, and Greece, and it's a fact that the most ancient Apostolic patriarchates there have always been Eastern Orthodox, then how can Rome be the 'Mother Church' and the Pope of Rome be the head of all churches?"

The question arose, like that of my future bride in a Kentucky convent school, in a review of church history. Our professor's desire was to impress upon us seminarians the fact that a wide diversity had, for centuries, existed side by side within the Roman Catholic communion. Another might have ignored the question, dismissed it as impertinent, or perhaps even silenced the inquirer. But that was not the style of this man, who was a scholar active in various historical associations.

"Charles, as you know from your own readings, that is one of the key questions still dividing East and West. It isn't an easy one, regardless of what either Church's catechisms say. The Holy scriptures affirm Peter as *kephas,* chief of the Apostles who were the first bishops. Rome may not have been first in foundation, but even the schismatic Churches of the East have always acknowledged Rome's primacy—although not the notion of supremacy—among the early Churches. Christ our Lord founded the Church in Jerusalem, and James, His step-brother, was the first bishop there. In fact, because of this, for the past couple of centuries Catholic-minded Anglicans and Lutherans have often proposed that Jerusalem, as the original 'Mother Church' of us all, be re-established as the center for a reunited Christendom. We also know that not only Rome was founded by the two leading Apostles, Peter and Paul: so was Antioch.

"So, once again, our history shows that Rome's primacy does not rest on being first in historical foundation. Our Church teaches that historical development in church orders and doctrine plays an important role in the life and structure of the Church. Rome, we teach, enjoys certain pontifical rights flowing from the foundation of Peter as head of the Apostles, and this developed as the Church matured. On these points, the Orthodox, the Anglicans, and even a number of European Roman Catholic and Eastern Rite authorities disagree with Rome, perhaps understandably so. Nevertheless, here in the seminary we teach the doctrines and canons of our Mother Church, which is Rome.

"An opportunity may come later when you can look into these questions that divide Christianity, East from West especially. I suggest you hold off until you get into the theologate, where the Church's theology, orders, and administration are the seminarian's major fields of study. Or if you're among the lucky few chosen—you might even get the chance to examine it first-hand at the Gregorian or Russicum College in Rome. For right now, though, take your time, my boy. Concentrate on your spiritual formation: you'll need it by the time you tackle Church doctrines and canon law in Theology."

Fair enough answer, it seemed at the time. But like Mary Ann's question, it would remain unresolved for a long time. Other questions of faith and church practice also raised their heads: the penchant of Rome and other Western churches to define even things which touched on the essence of God's own nature and at times to exalt Christ's mother, Mary, as "Co-Redemptrix"; Rome's medieval discipline of enforced celibacy, in contrast to the Apostolic and patristic norm of a married parish clergy, East and West alike; and the discrepancies in the Roman See's handling of moral and ethical issues—more dependent, it began to seem, on the individual Pope's situation and/or the secular influences during different eras in history than upon consistent Church teachings or pastoral action.

All of this served to add to my disquiet as a dutiful son of Rome, and the appeal of the Eastern Churches' traditions some-how became more conscious. My discovery of an anthology of Orthodox Russian philosopher Nikolai Berdyaev's reflections on faith and existence gave me additional food for thought.

Even so, the deciding factors for my eventual decision some time later to leave the seminary were primarily social and per-sonal. I felt the normal tugs of youthful emotions, indecision, and the attraction of the world, including a young male's normal desire to experience the wholesome company of young girls. Two of my closest seminary friends, including an upperclass role model, had earlier taken their leave for similar reasons. Return-ing home, in time I entered the nearby University of Florida and undertook studies toward a secular degree in political science.

This lasted just over a year. Inner turmoil and questioning as to whether I had honestly given the seminary a fair chance at my spiritual formation led me once more to take up the quest for the priesthood. I was accepted, on a trial basis, for candidacy as a Byzantine/Eastern Rites novice in the Jesuit order. The noviti-ate was devoted virtually entirely to spiritual formation and an intensive prayer life. It was there that I first discovered the

Eastern practice of the "Jesus Prayer", along with the discipline of the "Spiritual Exercises of St. Ignatius." My drift towards the Eastern Church became more definitely pronounced, but I was not to remain "Brother Charles, S.J." for very long. Before the year had passed, both the master of novices and I had concluded that even though the service of the Church remained a key (though as yet unexplainable) drive in my make-up, it was obvious that the Roman Catholic priesthood—whatever its way, shape, or locus—could not be my destiny.

In the meantime, Mary Ann had graduated from the convent school and, along with a schoolmate, accepted the F.B.I.'s offer of employment in Washington, D.C. An added attraction was the opportunity to enroll in the evening school of one of the local universities.

I left the Jesuit novitiate and moved back to my original hometown. A job offer as a "cub" reporter trainee materialized at the *Washington Star.* As with Mary Ann's situation, it also offered me the chance to continue college degree studies through a university evening school. Both of us fortuitously chose Georgetown University's excellent School of Foreign Service, under the administration of the Jesuit Fathers. We also chose the basic curriculum of political science and foreign languages, except that, for vague promptings which I did not at all understand then, I also continued to pursue religious studies on- and off-campus.

After two years, a vacancy opened up on the editorial staff of the *New York Herald Tribune's* Washington Bureau, and I eagerly took it. My duties were to assist the Washington editors, columnists, and news/editorial correspondents, to revamp the bureau's library and research capability, and to accept unspecified future assignments. This was to be my pursuit for nearly five years, up through the final years of the Eisenhower Administration and the historic 1960 Kennedy/Nixon debates and election.

It was an invaluable experience: to be there in the middle of the changing Washington political scene—no matter at what level, at the heart of a vibrant era in newspaper life, and to have the opportunity to meet and work and talk with many of the key people on all sides of the political spectrum. As time went on, the chance came, and—needless to say—was readily accepted, to assist in the researching and writing of timely works of political biographies and commentaries, as well as to help with the 1960 Democratic and Republican National Conventions in Los Angeles and Chicago. And all the while, I was able to pursue my studies and part-time training towards a degree in international public service and law. At that time, no one could have persuaded me—or the young co-ed from Kentucky whom I'd started dating—that my future life's work would be anything other than service as a newspaper correspondent or an overseas government officer.

Religiously speaking, before and after we came to meet each other at Georgetown University, both Mary Ann and I drifted during those years into casually experiencing faiths other than Rome's, including cultures very different from our own.

In the wake of the abortive Hungarian revolution against the Soviet occupation regime, I took to working as a volunteer with the "Assembly of Captive European Nations," an association modeled on the United Nations which comprised the exiled democratic leaders of nearly a dozen Eastern European countries that had fallen under Soviet Communist control after World War II. In turn, these activities brought me into further contact and knowledge of the Eastern churches, both the Orthodox and those subject to the See of Rome.

On the personal level, a somewhat rocky, on-again/off-again romance developed between Mary Ann and me, but we kept managing to come together ever more closely, in love and empathy, as time went on. The occasion of a research trip, which involved the writing of a book about key programs undertaken by the new Kennedy Administration, created the opportunity for our engagement early in 1961. So, Mary Ann Pearce and Charles Edward Wingenbach were wed in the tiny Roman Catholic church of "Our Lady of the Caves," in Cave City, Kentucky— ironically a mission of the formerly Protestant community which had been converted years before by the zealous Father Luigi!

We were not, however, destined to remain together for long at all: President John Kennedy had just resolved to call the Soviets' bluff in the crises over beleagured Berlin and Fidel Castro's Cuba. When the President and Secretary of Defense Robert McNamara announced that they would back up the U.S./Soviet confrontation with a military build-up, I discovered that my Naval Reserve unit, a small destroyer, was one of those being summoned back to active duty. My career and our new married life were shelved temporarily. I went off to anti-submarine and blockade patrol duty for the duration, and Mary Ann took up full-time employment with the District of Columbia Court in order to support herself and what infrequent family life we were able to have.

The Cuban missile confrontation brought the two super-powers and Cuba the closest the world has yet come to an all-out nuclear war. But once the crisis over Cuba and Berlin finally lessened in tension, the President released us several thousand Reservists to our normal civilian life.

Things were not the same, however. In the interim, the management of the *Herald Tribune* had changed hands and I— along with others on the newspaper's staff—chose, regretfully, to seek other employment. While still between jobs, the first of our four children, Mary-Adéle, was born just two days short of our first wedding anniversary. Providentially, a new job also mate-rialized, and I took up employment as a United States Senator's legislative/research assistant and in a "loaned" assignment in detail with President Kennedy's National Service task force.

"Somehow, our faith was still strong," Mary Ann remem-bers, "and—as always—God made up the difference. Even on the apparent brink of no income or a major crisis in our lives, we found that He has invariably held us up— *if* we but have faith to do our part in prayer and willingness to seek His will, not our own. Don't ask me to explain: it just happens that way, and it has so many times."

The work lasted just over a year, however, as it was cut short by the untimely mortal illness of the Senator. Once again, something came through. The success of my books on the twin themes of the Peace Corps and the American tradition of volun-teerism led to a contract offer, this time from one of the major publishers. The project involved Roman Catholic missionaries and volunteers in East Africa. It meant, however, another lengthy separation for us, as well as familiarizing myself with Swahili and the cultures of developing African peoples. The project completed late in 1963, I returned home to America, just in time for my wife to deliver Karl, our second child. I enlisted in work as a public relations consultant to the Governor of Ken-tucky and on detail with two state agencies.

The tragic death of President Kennedy had cut short the popular young Chief Executive's gradually developing National Service plans for an attack on America's domestic needs. However, his successor President Lyndon Johnson picked up the challenge, this time putting the full weight of the White House in support of the programs. In the Executive Office of the President, he assembled a bipartisan task force and began recruiting persons with experience in both the public and private sectors. As I had journalistic experience and had been associated with the formative stages of President Kennedy's Peace Corps and National Service projects, I was also recruited to work in the new President's innovative "Great Society" programs.

Mary Ann and I returned to Washington, and our third child, John, was born. During the years of 1965-1969, I was to criss-cross the country in a wide variety of community relations, training, volunteer development, and "trouble-shooting" assignments for the Executive Office's Economic Opportunity agency. The years spanned the Johnson Presidency, the troubled Sixties, and the initial year of the Nixon Administration.

We didn't realize it at the time, but the most decisive step we took in those years was in settling our religious orientation. Both Mary Ann and I felt that, especially with me being so much on the road, we had to find the stability of a real faith and religious grounding, centered in a community that we could appreciate together and in which we could confidently raise our young children. Following one of my initial whirlwind tours around America, while Mary Ann was at home with three small children, we started looking seriously. Mary-Adéle, Karl and John had been dutifully baptized as Christians in the Roman Catholic Church, but what we had experienced of the two nearby parishes of Rome's Latin Rite—Vatican II or not—left us cold.

One day we saw a feature in the *Washington Star* on the progress of a Ruthenian/Eastern Rite Catholic parish, which had not long before been established not far from us, in a former Protestant church building. We called the parish priest, and Father John came out to our home and told us all about St. Gregory of Nyssa Byzantine Catholic church and community. We sensed that in him we were meeting a caring pastor of souls, who was deeply devoted to the Church of his forefathers, an ancient but living community of faith and tradition. In time, we were drawn ever more deeply into learning to *live* the Church's mixed-language Liturgy, a communal worship experience which we entered into eagerly and fruitfully, for the first time in many years for both of us. We noticed that our three kids also seemed less restless and more "taken in". Essentially, our wanderings were finally over and our conversion had begun in earnest.

Father John was especially appreciative of my seminary training and varied experience. We became as active as we could, including in the church school and child-care programs and in the social-ethnic activities. Our request to transfer from Rome's Latin Rite to the Byzantine Catholic Church had to go all the way to the Vatican, but finally it was accepted. For us, that was a special day of rejoicing which we celebrated with Father John and friends at home. We offered our first "Service of the Blessing of the Breads" (that we later came to know as *Artoklasia,* in Greek) in thanksgiving together with the St. Gregory's community.

To our dismay, however, we soon discovered that the move to Byzantine Catholicism was misinterpreted: some family members and friends regarded us as having "deserted" our Roman Catholic heritage. Moreover, we increasingly observed that many leading Roman Catholic hierarchs and clergy viewed the Byzantine/Eastern Rites as somehow "not quite Catholic" enough for Roman tastes.

Such people were right in perceiving a real difference between the two traditions, because, as we later concluded, Byzantine Catholicism is the dubious heir within the Roman communion of the ancient Eastern Orthodox heritage of their forefathers. In a way, our critics were also correct in surmising that we were decisively going beyond the Roman Catholicism in which we had been raised. We did not know it at the time, nor were we by any means ready to go over to Orthodoxy then: all in God's own time.

It was a good while later, while functioning as a Byzantine Catholic religious educator and sometime ecumenical representative, that the choice was finally driven home. Chosen to participate in a regional Orthodox/Catholic retreat and seminar, I was the lone Byzantine Catholic representative. I found myself literally as well as figuratively in the middle, between the two great Church traditions. I discovered that I regularly sided with the

Orthodox in the discussions, since by now I had begun to resolve many of the doctrinal and ethical questions which had arisen in my youthful seminary days—and mostly not in Rome's favor, either. At the time, the Melkite and Ukrainian Catholic patriarchates' increasing confrontations with the Roman Curia, as well as the recent conversion to Orthodoxy of the Ruthenian Catholic Archdiocese's erudite young Chancellor[1] were very much in the news. The questions which they—and the Byzantine Catholic fathers at Vatican II—had conscientiously posed, concerning Rome's basic intentions with regards to the Eastern Churches and Orthodoxy, came up in the course of the conversations.

One of the Jesuit fathers, reform-minded but firmly Roman in outlook, took exception on these matters. He suggested that they were part of a larger problem, which he felt the Vatican ought to end as an admitted ecumenical "embarrassment". He then called for either the dismantling of the Roman Church's Eastern Rites and their consequent absorption into the indigenous churches of the Latin Rite, or—like it or not—for ceding them back to the Eastern and Oriental Orthodox Churches.

I was stunned and dismayed: so much for the "ancient rights and rites of the venerable Eastern Churches," which Rome had for the last century or so been trumpeting in defense against the claims of independent Orthodoxy! No theologian yet was I, but I had previously felt that the generous ecumenical spirit of the late Pope John XXIII was fairly reflective of Roman Catholicism's basic attitude towards diversity within her communion. Now, judging by the reactions which the Melkite and Ukrainian churches' criticisms had provoked in the Curia and by the consensus which the Jesuit theologian's remarks had met within the Roman Catholic delegation present in the dialogues, I began to surmise that his assessment represented his Church's stance more truly than did any of Pope John XXIII's or Vatican II's official decrees.

During the break in the final sessions of the dialogue, the senior Eastern Orthodox representative, Father John Tavlarides of Washington's St. Sophia Cathedral, suggested that we go for a quiet walk and conversation.

---

[1] Later to become Bishop John (Martin) of Nyssa, of the Carpatho-Russian Orthodox Diocese of America. † May his memory be eternal!

"Please understand, " he began earnestly, "I do not prose-lytize, and I'm not trying to proselytize you, either. But I saw your obvious dismay in there. I think you ought to realize that Father Charles, in his own inimitable way, was simply 'speaking the truth in love,' as the Apostle tells us to do. I have a question for you, my friend: if you walk like a duck, if you talk like a duck, if you prefer the ways of a duck, and if you act just like a duck, then, tell me, *shouldn't you really be a duck?* In other words, the way I see it, you're reaching the point where you have to become one or the other, yet you are still trying to be some sort of platypus!"

The point was made and well-taken. I began to realize that for me to try to be contented as a Byzantine Catholic layman, loyal regardless to Rome, would ultimately be indulging in self-deception and illusion. Challenged on both sides, I could give neither myself nor anyone else a satisfactory answer.

Mary Ann well remembers the pain, too, that I felt when, despite Rome's unilateral pronouncements to the contrary, I discovered that I could not after all receive Holy Communion with my Orthodox "brethren." When I came home from that weekend, she demanded that we bundle up the kids and go out for a picnic in Rock Creek Park, expecting that I would at last unburden myself of it all. She was right, as she almost invariably is intuitively. We had come to know each other, in many ways "mind and soul". We walked, played with our children, and sat and talked for hours, even after returning home; then we went on well into the night and part of the next day.

A decision had begun to take shape. Why, then, was the final act of formal conversion delayed to another year? Looking back, we are now convinced that the time simply wasn't ripe. We prayed, we read more deeply into the sources of both traditions, communed more frequently in the Sacraments, and shared some of our thoughts and anguish with Father John. He counseled us to more prayer, but naturally could not settle the question for us.

Another factor also intervened: the rude reception that Mary Ann and I had meanwhile experienced at the hands of lay leaders of a very ethnic Orthodox parish. Desirous of drawing closer and hoping even to learn as a family, we applied to enroll our three children in their Orthodox day-school. The institution turned out to be more "parochial" than we had imagined possible, for despite the endorsement of the parish priest there we ran into a sharp, unfriendly rebuff. School enrollment, we were finally informed, was strictly limited to children of that ethnic heritage. It was also the very first time we would hear the term *xenos,* which we discovered is often used by some ethnic-centered and inhospitable Greeks to refer to "foreigners"; that is, "people not like us."* Where had we heard that sentiment before? Unfortunately, it was not to be the last time we would hear it.

Nonetheless, it was but a temporary setback, and also a valuable, sobering learning experience. We saw Orthodoxy and the Church in more realistic terms. We realized that, regardless of the faith shared, "the grass is not necessarily greener on the other side of the fence." It has been our experience that far too many converts are captivated by the beauty and meaning of life that they find in the Orthodox Liturgy, as well as the ideal state of the Kingdom which they read about in, for example, Timothy Ware's[2] or the late Nicholas Zernov's writings—but somehow sidestep the historical, human realities and frailties which those very same authors pointed out. Then, when they encounter an experience such as ours, they tend to become extremely judgmental or swiftly disillusioned critics of Orthodoxy and the "institutional" Church. They and, paradoxically, many so-called 'traditionalist' Orthodox somehow fail to realize that our Lord *inaugurated* the Kingdom on this earth; He didn't finish it up for us, and the warts as well as the beauty marks appear on the face of the Church.

At the same time as the beginning of our final transition into Orthodoxy, other factors were coming to a head in our lives. I was experiencing more and more disquiet in my life and work. Both Mary Ann and I sensed the tension in the air, and sometimes it overtook us. We realized that, if not faced up to and resolved, the underlying turmoil could even wreck the marriage and home that we had been blessed with and which we mutually cherished. Part of the disquiet was traceable to tensions over matters of principle and ethical behavior which, early as it was,

* *It also means 'guest,' but in this case it was clearly meant to exclude. Ed.*

[2] Now Bishop Kallistos of Diokleia, auxiliary to the Archbishop of Thyateira and Great Britain. A convert from Anglicanism, he is an Orthodox ecumenical and missionary leader.

had already begun to surface within the Nixon Administration. So far as we were concerned, something had to give, and *soon*.

That "something" was the career and life in Washington, D.C. The occasion for a decision was the more or less simultaneous offer of two jobs: one, a higher-level position in another Federal government agency office in Washington, which would have meant a closer involvement with certain Administration officials whom Mary Ann and I regarded as dubious characters, at best; the other was a challenging and innovative, but lower-paying, interagency position away from Washington, in Oak Ridge, Tennessee. Our recollections of the dilemma are vivid, even to this day.

We prayed and talked, but deep down we knew what we had to do anyway. Staying in Washington could easily mean surrendering our sense of one another and our most basic ideals about how things are done in this world. Staying, we are both convinced, would have written a disastrous chapter in our lives; God only knows what would have happened. It was hard to give up comfortable living, friends, associations, and career interests, but we could do no other.

The formal act of conversion soon followed on the steps of the move to Oak Ridge, located some twenty or so miles from Knoxville, Tennessee. A friendly and receptive parish priest and church community in Knoxville clinched the matter. Our whole family at the time — Mary Ann and I, Mary-Adéle, Karl and John — were chrismated in St. George Greek Orthodox Church on the Sunday of Orthodoxy, 1970, at the hands of Father George Pantelis.[3] Presbytera Vicky was our *koumbara* or sponsor.

Not one to let opportunities go to waste, Father George recruited his new converts: I as Religious Education teacher, and later supervisor and youth advisor; Mary Ann with the Philoptochos Ladies Auxiliary; and the three children became regulars in the Sunday School's elementary division. A close bond and identification rapidly grew between the Pantelis and Wingenbach families, as well as with other families and parishioners of the community. The entry of our family and other newcomers into

---

[3] Father George's life and devoted pastoral ministry were tragically cut short by an assassin's bullets, in the Annunciation Church of Buffalo, New York on the Feast of the Holy Cross of Christ, September 1979. † May his memory be eternal!

parish life also strengthened Father George's resolve to broaden the congregational use of Greek and English in the services. After the historic 1970 Archdiocese Clergy-Laity Congress, when the local option for the use of English in the Liturgy and sacraments was expanded, the ingenious pastor also saw the need for help, if he were to undertake it well.

It was only natural that in discussing my background in seminary and continuous religious activities, the idea of the priesthood would resurface. And so it did alike to Father George and me. Still, when it actually did come out into the open, we were both startled. It was for me the beginning of my adult pilgrimage into priestly ministry.

Once again, there had to be the right occasion, "else the seed will not fall upon good ground." The occasion was Archbishop Iakovos' announcement that Patriarch Athenagoras and the Mother Church of Constantinople had approved his proposal for an auxiliary corps of deacons and priests, manned by men who would continue in their lay professions, yet who would help the Church part-time in the Divine Services and ministries of her regional districts and local parishes.

Father George proposed my name to Archbishop Iakovos and Bishop Aimilianos, who was the Archdiocesan auxiliary for the Southern diocesan district at the time. The idea was warmly received and seconded, almost to her own amazement, by Mary Ann and by the St. George parish council leaders.

Meanwhile, the actual fact of our young family's conversion to Eastern Orthodoxy had been received with mixed feelings—and, in some cases, coolly—by our relatives. Some wondered just how stable or sincere this change was on my own and Mary Ann's part. Mary Ann's mother, Mrs. Mary Clark Pearce, recalls that she was relieved to find that we hadn't turned into fanatics, and both of us and the children seemed happier and more settled as a result. Of course, she was hurt because we seemed to be turning our backs on so much of what was precious to her and our life together. But her husband Bill advised a wait-and-see attitude.

"You may not believe this," Mrs. Pearce said later, "but what made us truly feel at ease, even to rejoice, was to hear that Chuck was going to become a priest. We were happy that Mary Ann was happy and at ease about it, too. You could see there was always something of the priest in Chuck, trying to get out. I felt right away that he'd come home to what, deep down, he and God wanted him to be and do. At least for Bill and me, that settled it. The experience of attending his ordination as a deacon in Knoxville is still a fond, beautiful memory. Besides, we fell in love with Father George and we were convinced that Chuck and Mary Ann and the kids were in good hands there."

The reaction was virtually the same on the part of my own aged mother,* who was then semi-retired at our old Florida family homestead.

In time, a program of painstaking, gradual spiritual formation, bilingual liturgical training, and various academic courses were worked out between the Archbishop, Bishop Aimilianos, Holy Cross Seminary, Father George, and me. Complete weekends and, whenever possible, weekdays and evenings were carved out of the busy schedules of the pastor and his candidate. Occasional part-time residencies, visits, and regular study assignments at the Seminary were developed with two of the faculty and supervised locally by Father George.

The day came when the sub-diaconal and cantorial training was judged sufficient. On the Sunday before Christmas, 1971, Charles Edward Wingenbach formally became Father Deacon Gregory Charles Wingenbach, in my home parish of St. George's in Knoxville. I had taken the patristic name of Gregory (of Nyssa) in love of St. Basil's younger brother who had likewise experienced vocational struggles and in gratitude for the "bridge" role which our former Byzantine Catholic parish in Washington had — by God's design — played in our pilgrimage as a family to Orthodoxy.

For nearly two years more, I interned as new pastoral assistant, sometimes even while on the road as program officer for the consortium of government agencies and Southern universities which employed me. On these visits to other cities around the country, I took every opportunity I could to meet and serve with local priests or bishops in different liturgical settings, and mostly in Greek. By late 1972, I had also completed a Bachelor's degree in Eastern Christian Spirituality, reversing my former

* Since departed † May her memory be eternal.

94

"minor" in religious studies to become the "major" of my new academic pursuits.

By early 1973, it was apparent that the new program had in this instance worked not only to the satisfaction of all concerned, but also that the Archdiocese's, the Bishop's, Father George's, and my own interest in my priestly ministry had mutually deepened.

The trouble was that I was, by now, putting in sixty or more hours each week in town and on the road in the management of my agency responsibilities, and often on top of that as many as twenty hours each week in my theological studies, priestly training, and auxiliary ministry with St. George's parish. Excepting the increased time that as a family we were spending together in-church, our home and family life was running the risk of being sidetracked.

Once again, something had to give. With the concurrence of Mary Ann, Bishop Aimilianos and Father George agreed that the time had come to recommend to Archbishop Iakovos that the Deacon be finally prepared and ordained as a priest—on condition, though, that I resign my secular career and undertake graduate seminary training and further pastoral internship.

Mary Ann and I had had in mind that, somehow, I should go to finish up at Holy Cross and work meanwhile in an internship-assistancy with one or more of the nearby New England parishes. But the Archbishop, who had summoned me to New York, had an entirely different idea. In his paternal concern, His Eminence wanted to take no chances that I should fail or that the auxiliary-ministry program itself should be jeopardized. He informed me that I was being sent to Greece for my program, and a special graduate curriculum would be worked out there to train me finally for the regular priestly ministry.

"It will be better for you if you experience the priestly life and undertake your courses of study back in the Motherland itself," His Eminence directed. "There you will have the chance to learn your Greek. By knowing and experiencing more of the basic traditions of Greek Orthodoxy firsthand—better than your future parishioners themselves, in most cases—you will be able, my son, to deal with the challenges of being a parish priest among us."

That meant, in obedience, that we had to change our lives around completely. We sold everything we had, including the home in Oak Ridge, and Mary Ann and the kids had to move in with her family back in Louisville, Kentucky for the duration of my studies overseas. I would be living in a monastery and attending a Greek university seminary. The latter seemed the greatest hurdle, given my lack of knowledge of all but the liturgical Greek. But, once again, we knew the Lord would provide, and provide He did.

On the Fifth Sunday of Lent, April 1973, I became Father Gregory, fully a priest of the Archdiocese and the Ecumenical See, and ironically, in the northern Florida parish of another convert-priest, Father James Laliberte, who joined the Bishop and Father George in welcoming me as a brother in Christ. This time, my proud and happy Roman Catholic mother and family members were able to join Mary Ann and me and the kids in sharing that special milestone in our lives.

The internship in Greece was, by any yardstick, a fruitful one, though the country was racked by two revolutions at the time. The spoken Greek came to me *etsi kai etsi,* so-so. At the University of Thessaloniki and the Patriarchal Institute of the ancient Vlatadon Monastery, I concentrated on studies of pastoral theology and practices, liturgics, development in Church traditions, and various works of early Church Fathers. Aside from a brief field trip to Epiros in Religious Education, my field internship was as co-chaplain of two communities in the Thessaloniki Archdiocese, together with Father Eugene Pappas, previously an overseas missionary in Asia for the American Archdiocese. We operated under the sponsorship and assignment of the then-Metropolitan Archbishop of Thessaloniki, popularly called "Pater Leonidas"[4], who became a spiritual father, role model, and close friend who much influenced us both. Visits to Mt. Athos, Sparta, and the Ecumenical Patriarchate in Turkey deepened my own appreciation of Orthodoxy's spiritual life and "core" traditions. And only once, in Athens, did I encounter prejudice and the hostile epithet *"xenos".*

[4] This beloved 'pastor of pastors,' later removed from his See during political upheavals surrounding the Greek-Turkish-Cyprus crisis, met his Maker during Holy Week 1984, in an automobile accident, while on an errand of mercy. His last will bequeathed all that he had: books, vestments, etc. to the Orthodox missions and to the Church's spiritual renewal movement in Greece. † May his memory be eternal!

Returning to America, I was quickly given a regular assignment as a missionary priest in the South, serving as pastor first in Louisville, Kentucky and then in Nashville, Tennessee, for a period totalling nine years. In the meantime, thanks to the continuing support and encouragement of the Archbishop, I was also enabled to complete my Master's and Doctoral degrees in Pastoral and Ecumenical Theology. At the request and assignment of His Grace Bishop Maximos of Pittsburgh, early in 1983, I was installed as pastor of the nearby Monessen (PA) community, plus in particular Diocesan and Archdiocesan responsibilities.

While still in Louisville, in 1978 Presbytera Mary Ann delivered our fourth child, Evgenia Kisa Maria: both of them, thanks be to God, managed to come through critical life-threatening illnesses in the process. Our family was now complete: also thanks to God, our two eldest children, Mary-Adéle and Karl, successfully completed their undergraduate college degrees and basic career training, while John is pursuing his science college major toward completion.

Also complete was our conversion process, or pilgrimage in faith. Prior to our actual chrismation, as the above story recounts, we had come ever closer to Orthodoxy, much of the time without hardly realizing it was happening. We were seeking a community which, with all of the obvious warts of its human members and institutions, has steadfastly mirrored the community of faith and love which Christ promised to His disciples and the believing world.

Mary Ann and I, and—we hope—our children as well, have seen in Orthodoxy, East and West, a timeless communion that is unbroken in its fidelity to Christ's promise, to the New Covenant which He established with His apostles. In the holy Eucharistic Liturgy and Sacraments, we basically experience the healing power and grace that only God can give. So, more than ever do we hunger and pray for the union of all Christians, for "broken yet never sundered apart is the body of Christ," as we pray just before receiving Holy Communion.

We have come to see each other, our children, and others as icons of the Lord Himself, Who made us as His very own *eikones,* mirroring His own image and likeness. Yet, like the paint and wood and gesso of the material icon, we have our imperfections. And we experience those imperfections in ourselves, in the society we live in, and within the very institutions of our Church. Among those imperfections—which mar and distort God's image before others—we can readily perceive our Church's inability to seriously face up to Christ's Great Commission. And that Commission is to become as One . . . to seek to serve and help and love others . . . and to reach out seriously to many, many others who, like us, have experienced inner hunger for something more and who are still searching for hope and love in Orthodoxy's family of Christ's faithful.

As one convert told his fellow parish council members some years ago while I was the pastor of a struggling, sometimes divided parish community, "Do you realize how *hard* it is to get past the obstacles, in order to actually become Orthodox? The welcomes often aren't there at the local level; and the ethnic divisions and fractured 'witness' of the SCOBA[5] council of America's Orthodox bishops and jurisdictions just don't tend to inspire you to run that gauntlet. Sometimes, it makes it nigh impossible for us to find in modern Orthodoxy that 'pearl of great price' that Father Gregory and I have, by the grace of God, found. What a terrible burden it must be for someone, if he or she is the 'stone of scandal' that prevents another, sincere seeker after the truth from coming in. I'd hate to have that burden, let me tell you."

We know only too well what that person was feeling and what he was talking about. Still, we've always been able to find consolation and strength in Christ, no matter what. As persons and as a priestly family, we continue to have our ups and downs. It isn't easy. But after all, God *did* promise us a "rose garden", and we all know that roses have thorns as well as beauty and a soothing fragrance.

After all these years, we thank God that, in all the important things, we come to a sense of peace now. We know who we are. We know where we are. We don't know where the future will take us, God willing. We do know that, mostly *together*, we've come a long, long way.

---

[5] Standing Conference of Canonical Orthodox Bishops in the Americas. The body includes the following jurisdictions: the Albanian Orthodox Diocese of America, the American Carpatho-Russian Orthodox Greek Catholic Diocese in the U.S.A., the Antiochian Orthodox Christian Archdiocese of North America, the Bulgarian Eastern Orthodox Church, the Greek Orthodox Archdiocese of North and South America, the Orthodox Church in America, the Romanian Orthodox Missionary Archdiocese in America and Canada, the Serbian Orthodox Church in the U.S.A. and Canada, and the Ukrainian Orthodox Church in America.

Encounters with Orthodoxy: Two Anecdotes

*   *   *   *   *

I Must Decrease: He Must Increase
by Victoria Smith

It was a bitter cold February evening. The silver crescent of a moon shone thinly on snow that squeaked beneath my feet as I walked from the village center. The train station bisected the shopping district from the residential, and I was heading home-ward. I vividly recall how dispirited I had been. I had many material things, and yet I had nothing! I had a well-paying job in investment banking which supplied my wants and my needs, the luxuries by which the world says, "You're on your way." I had "nothing" because the pleasure derived from achieving died in its own satisfaction. I was aware of a great longing but did not know then for what.

Eighteen years earlier I felt called out and broke with family tradition. God seemed to say, "I will offer you something better." But I was in the desert. I was interpreting God's call to His way of life as something I had to *do,* whereas in reality, it was something I had to *be.* During childhood I was nurtured on the Word of God, and had a child's faith in God. I grew, but my faith remained one-dimensional. I was taught to be kind, to be giving, to be helpful, and to avoid evil by doing good. But this shallow activism in adult life neglected the discipline of prayer and the discipline of penitence. Now most denominations in the Christian faith will incorporate prayer in varying degrees, but penitence? Therein lies the defect. St. John the Baptist said, "Bear fruit that befits repentance." (Matthew 3:8) My faith had dwindled to a token worship because it had no expression either intellectually or heart-felt. Life was devoid of enrichment.

Salty tears sprang up and quickly froze on my cold cheeks. The late commuter train was just pulling in with its burden of weary breadwinners. "It's all for naught," I thought, and without hesitation and explanation I stepped onto the track into the brightness of the engine's light! The shock of the blast of the diesel horn so startled me, I instinctively jumped off the track-bed.

I walked away toward the light of a shop across the street. My knees were shaking as I entered and asked the proprietors if I could sit down. The older couple thought I was just cold and quickly produced a cup of hot coffee.

Since I brought my clothes to them for tailoring, I knew Peter and Lilly slightly. They had come to America before World War II, he from Mytilene, she from Athens. They were warm-hearted, loving, and hospitable, and they gave to me, in the days ahead, a home life I had lost.

Early in the week of April 6, 1969, I stopped into the shop after work. They were closing early, because it was Holy Week and the Bishop was coming to the Tuesday night service. Peter very naturally said, "Want to come with us?"

Forty days earlier, shortly after that fateful night, I had gone with them to a Mardi Gras costume dance in the church hall, but had never seen the church, nor had expressed anything but surprise to find I lived only two blocks away. Not having anything else to do, I easily replied "yes". We shared a sparse supper and with them I entered a small dimly lighted rustic church. I sat between them in the third pew.

Peter nodded to a portly man in a black robe standing to the left and said, "My brother Elias . . . the chanter."

"Where's the altar?" I wondered. I recognized the throne as such, but what is this wall of paintings? I automatically reached for a book in the pew rack. I couldn't read the writing! I put it back.

Suddenly there was a burst of action: part of the wall in front moved away, revealing an altar, Bishop, and priest. Men spilled forth from doors in the wall and stood around Elias. The chanting began and, on occasion, the Bishop across the nave took his turn. I didn't understand a word but entered into the spirit of the service. The congregation, as I recall, was passive. The action was all played out before us. The lighted candles increased in number, like exclamation points for the chanting, as worshippers moved about throughout the service. The incense filled the little church, seeming to envelope us in a cloud of angelic spirits. I fervently called to mind all the lines of the penitential psalms I could draw on, as it seemed fitting for the occasion. Something was stirring within me; I felt a joy even among all that was strange and wonderful! I went home that night hoping to return.

How can one outside the Orthodox faith, having no prior knowledge of its existence, be adequately prepared for the spiritual impact of the Anastasis service and Divine Liturgy? From my earliest days, the Lord Jesus Christ was made a very real part of my life. Faithful church attendance was a delight more than a duty. But the processions and pageantry of those services pale in the glorious splendor of the unwaning Light of the Resurrection. I don't recall any English spoken that first Pascha, but I do remember the drama of the suspenseful darkness, the sombre chanting, then an auroral flickering above the iconostasis before the coming out of the Royal Doors of the Paschal Light. Understanding transcends language at this moment. One sees the Resurrection banner in procession, receives the light, hears the joyous proclamation, *"Christos anesti ek nekron . . . !"*

I was there! I had arrived only at the eleventh hour, but as St. John Chrysostom says, "He gives rest to him who comes at the eleventh hour as well as to him that has toiled from the first . . . Let all then enter into the joy of our Lord."

It was a night to remember. I received a red egg, the red signifying the Blood of Christ, its shell His three-day entombment, and its breaking His Resurrection, bringing forth new life. The congregation then gathered in the pre-dawn hours for a lamb dinner, breaking their seven-week fast. This was my introduction to the Orthodox phronema.*

The following Sunday, and every Sunday thereafter by myself, I went to Divine Liturgy. It was a testing of my sincerity, because the numbers of church-goers I had encountered initially rapidly diminished and disappeared altogether by June. Oddly, only a handful of elderly, and myself, were in church during that first summer; on one very humid Sunday morning, I was the only one along with the chanter and priest! I wondered greatly.

In the few months following Easter, I was like the proverbial moth drawn to the flame. I was stirred up, excited by the

---

* *Mind, thought, view, or spirit. From the Greek.*

discovery of a worship service that quickened my spirit through the externals that I could understand. My life took on an added dimension. God was drawing me to Himself.

In September church membership and activity resumed. There appeared in the pew racks bilingual Divine Liturgy books, and I eagerly read the English translation of the prayers and the short explanations of what I had been witnessing without understanding. Then I tackled the language. I found the Greek alphabet in the dictionary and memorized the letters and their sounds. Each Sunday I would listen to the priest chant and word by word, since it is slower than speaking, I learned the Liturgy in Greek. I recognized that the Orthodox Liturgy flows right from Scripture, from the Psalms, and the Old and New Testaments.

I took my next step. I joined the choir. The music was very strange to my ear, and I first found it quite difficult, but I was determined to persist. Singing praises to God is a fundamental expression of worship and a vehicle for spiritual growth in the liturgical life. I wanted to experience more fully the corporate life of the Church and was encouraged to do so by some of the members.

For a while the exhilaration of the involvement in discovering a spiritual home sustained me, but a frustration gnawed away at me. I was listening to, and mouthing, words I did not understand. I was making the motions, catching the undertone, but I was unable to develop a God relationship in Orthodoxy due to my language limitations. I couldn't understand the Scripture readings nor the sermon. I voiced my frustration one day to a born-Orthodox, and he startled me with the revelation, "We don't understand the Liturgical Greek, either!" He confessed to attending Greek School and Sunday School, "But we never learned what it was all about because we couldn't understand the language!"

I went home and wept. "They've embalmed Jesus, not embodied Him!"

What was I to do?

There comes a time when each person has the responsibility to find out for himself what the Truth is. Obviously, some people will start at one point and others at a totally different one. Some, due to the accident of birth, will be exposed to one line of thinking more readily than others, and for these things they are not responsible, but they are responsible to examine the evidence available to them and work assiduously to arrive at the Truth. Faith is not a natural, instinctive characteristic, and compliance with it is not automatic. Faith is first a gift from God, then an achievement; it is a way of life, a guiding principle for the whole personality. I decided to trust that God would work it out.

A new pastor arrived to shepherd the flock. A new dimension was given to us. We were not to look for church membership and church "activity" but were to seek the reality of Christ in our lives! Fr. Kallistos used both Greek and English in all worship services. He translated and printed for our edification many of the services, the lives of the saints, and a dictionary of Orthodox terminology.

Have you ever seen a desert bloom? I've been to the Holy Land many times. After the winter rains, the once arid hills are alive with red and yellow flowers that spring up and blossom overnight. So it was with us! Hearing the Word of God, and understanding, we blossomed, we multiplied, we discovered Christ in our midst. I absorbed it all. I learned we had a seminary nearby, and a bookstore. I read the Church Fathers, the Desert Fathers, the lives of the saints, books on the Liturgy, the Sacraments, the Creed, Orthodox Church history. The more I learned the more I realized what a great treasure of spirituality was within the Orthodox Church. I discovered the true God: Holy, Almighty, and Immortal. When I responded, *Kyrie, eleison,* it was with a humility the Eastern Fathers recognized in composing the Liturgy's litanies, as the most perfect prayer. Why? Because they understood the transcendence of God and man's own littleness and complete dependence on Him. Like the publican in the synagogue, we can only stand, head bowed, before our God, and say, "Lord, have mercy on me, the sinner!"

But I was still not a communicant! For two-and-a-half years I faithfully attended every Sunday. The congregation gradually had become used to my attendance, and I gave my support to all the functions of the church. I don't know what they thought, if at all, of my faithful participation as a non-Orthodox. There were no adult instruction classes, which is the door to membership in other Christian denominations, and I was not married to an Orthodox, so an invitation to join the church just never materialized. The subject was never brought up. In-

103

volvement in activities focused on social fund-raisers. My study of the Orthodox faith was pursued privately through my purchase of books. To have asked questions would have caused embarrassment, for in reality, we were learning together under Fr. Kallistos's shepherding. I felt that God had brought me this close, and yet I could not partake of His Divine Nature. So I started to pray with all My heart, "Lord, save me; I perish!"

The Lord, in His own time and in His own way, answered my prayers. But not as expected!

I became ill and was hospitalized.

The doctor said, "You have cancer. We'll operate tomorrow!"

It was a couple of months before I could return to the church. I made a thank offering of a chanter's stand for the church.

Fr. Kallistos said, "Victoria, wouldn't you like to become an Orthodox Christian?"

"Oh, very much so. I thought you'd never ask!"

I was chrismated on March 12, 1972, midst a rejoicing congregation who became my brothers and sisters in Christ.

In analyzing my journey to Christ through conversion to the Orthodox faith, I would describe it as a continuation of a journey but a climb at the upper levels. I was born into a Christian home and the journey started at an early age. But the road became choked with life's experiences during the Forties, Fifties and Sixties of this century, and I meandered. In what could very well be a testing, or even a method to bring my relationship with God to maturity, God withholds His response to immature expression. He takes away the "toys" — the warm "fuzzies" — the pleasurable self-satisfaction in "good deeds". It seems to me, as I look back on those "desert" days, that feeling the absence of God I had to grow firmer in faith and hope. I felt called out to seek a deeper experience of God, but it was not to be given to me readily. There was a mountain to climb, a need for the unclean garment of my life to be purified. I was to struggle, and still do. Indeed, the deeper one goes into the Word of God, the greater the struggle becomes because of the Spirit's conviction.

I wavered in my hope but, praise the Lord, He had better plans. I must live in the power of the Holy Spirit, not taking the

Spirit for granted, but in a holy fear. I must give myself to whatever God wishes and for as long as He wishes. There is never a moment when there is not some virtue to be practised. And I can't know these things without reading and discussion. This is why I am impelled to study. At one moment God gives me the desire to instruct myself in what, at a later moment, will help me to act virtuously. But whatever I do, I do it because I am drawn to this particular action without knowing why. I can only say, I feel drawn to write, to read, to question and examine. I obey this feeling and God, Who is responsible for it. This builds up within me a kind of spiritual store which will develop into a core of usefulness for myself and for others.

I avail myself of every opportunity, when it does not conflict with my present work, to attend the many and varied worship services which make up the daily Divine Offices offered by my parish priest throughout any given week. The opportunity is given to truly live immersed in the Orthodox life of prayer, fasting, and communion with God. These are the riches of the faith which none other can approach in comparability. From the awesome depths to the ecstatic heights, God is with us.

It may be easier to live a life in another religious persuasion, but Orthodoxy is the Faith easier to die in. In the crises of life no other gift is so essential as faith in God. And when God grants the gift of the Orthodox faith, you are receiving the purest, the loftiest, the truest expression of the Apostolic Faith within the Body of Christ.

"Come, taste and see how sweet the Lord is!"

*　　　*　　　*　　　*　　　*

"Entering the Church"
by Susan McShane

My brother Mike and I were raised as Methodists. We were not active in church events. Our mother, who had a hard job raising two children by herself after our father's death, was not strict about church attendance and allowed us to decide when we wanted to attend. Mike and I attended church with our maternal grandfather, but I remember stopping after he died. Mike stopped one year before. I mean no disrespect, but I never felt anything special, as I do now.

In 1971 Michael met a lovely Greek-American girl named Helen at college and started attending the Annunciation Cathedral in Baltimore. He went to the dances as well as the Adult Sunday School. He grew to like the church and its traditions.

Through his involvement in the church, our mother and I were invited to attend some of the events. That's when I became interested in the church. When I was there, I felt good and welcomed by the people, and had a feeling of belonging even though I had not converted yet.

Mike's chrismation was in 1976. My mother and I went to the church to observe the event. The chrismation was a lovely ceremony. I watched with great interest. I watched the people around me, the chanters, who added much to the ceremony. I could see most of the people who had come for the liturgy and realized that everyone had accepted Mike with open arms.

Six months later Helen and Mike were married. I was a bridesmaid in the wedding. I think it was the wedding, and not only its beauty, that really convinced me to convert.

Mike had been in a motorcycle accident one month before, luckily breaking only two bones in his foot. By the date of the wedding, he needed to use a cane and his foot was still swollen. He had to buy two pairs of dress boots, one pair size seven for his left foot and one size nine for his right. But what to do with the cane during the ceremony?

He held the cane in his right hand, but it was visible to the people in the pews. Later, our mother said that she heard someone behind her ask what the cane was for and that maybe it was part of Greek wedding traditions.

Right from the start, the family and friends of the wedding party were involved with the rehearsal and the actual plans of the wedding. Helen looked beautiful and radiant, and Mike was as handsome as ever. After the ushers and bridesmaids were in place at the altar, we waited for Mike and Helen to come together at the steps that would bring them to the solea. What made the greatest impression on me was when the families kissed the bride and the groom.

I guess to me it just showed that there was no drawing back on the part of Helen's family from the fact that their daughter or granddaughter was marrying someone who was not Greek. There was complete acceptance and, most importantly, love on the part of both families. Our family did not care that Helen was not Irish, either. Possibly it was that both families realized that Mike and Helen loved each other, as there now is love between both families.

This was the first Greek wedding I had attended. The ceremony was beautiful and the chanters seemed to take away the tension I felt in standing up in front of a lot of people.

With Mike's increasing interest in Helen and the Church, my Mom and I were invited to the church for different events. From my being in the church and around Father Constantine I felt I belonged and welcome, but I wanted to make sure that my decision to become Greek Orthodox was not just a whim. I attended some of the liturgies on my own.

Something was missing from my life, I knew, and after a great deal of thought I realized that it was religion. I set up an appointment to talk to a priest to make sure my commitment was strong. Father Mark, a very intelligent man, listened as I told him how I felt and what I had done to finally make my decision. In turn, Father Mark told me that he felt my commitment was strong.

I was chrismated on October 21, 1979. My oldest niece, Corinna, was also christened then.

I don't know how anyone else feels after witnessing a christening in an Orthodox church, but it seems that everyone takes the ceremony privately with its own meaning. Afterward, some people are very happy and talkative and hugging and kissing, while others, just as happy, are quiet and walk around the Cathedral, taking in the warmth and quiet of the church.

When christenings are held in our Cathedral, there is one thing I like to do when everyone has gone downstairs to the social hall for the dinner or small family luncheon. When I think that there isn't anyone upstairs in the Cathedral, I go up there by myself and just walk around inside. I don't think I can describe the warmth I feel. Maybe it's the feeling that everyone close to you has come together to celebrate the continuation of the family, of life. I feel close to God just walking around and looking at the icons and the stained glass windows, at the beauty of the Cathedral.

There are beautiful works of man-made art throughout the entire Cathedral: the icons, stained glass windows, the altar, the marble. But really, the other part of the Cathedral is the people, who make the Cathedral work, who reflect what our Cathedral really stands for: family and love. Over the past five years I still see the feeling for family and the love for one's church.

Both are equally important. The people need the Cathedral and the Cathedral needs the people. I have a strong feeling about the many young children in our Cathedral, too. Even though they are too young to vote anyone into office, they aren't excluded from any part of the Cathedral. They attend Sunday School and liturgy every Sunday. Father Constantine often talks to the parents about how important it is for the children to attend Sunday School.

But from what I see when the children are going to Sunday School, I think the parents would enroll their children in school, anyway. I think that the families talk and teach the children about how important it is to go to church and how important it is to believe in one's religion. The children don't cry about being brought to church, but come because they want to. From what I know about the families of our Cathedral, I feel that the children are taught love and respect for their elders, their religion, and their Cathedral.

I said *their* Cathedral, because it is our Cathedral, not just a building that sits on a corner of two streets. It is the second home for people who have started families, where memories are made and people can learn about and practice their religion.

Odyssey to Orthodoxy[1]

by Rt. Reverend Gordon Thomas Walker

Though raised in a devout Christian home, my own spiritual odyssey began in earnest when, at age 10, I "walked the aisle" of the Baptist Church of Pinson, Alabama, and gave my heart to Christ. Shortly thereafter, I was baptized in the name of the Father, Son, and Holy Spirit in a very cold stream known as Turkey Creek. Later, at age 16, at a youth revival (as they are called in the South) in my home church in Palmerdale, Alabama, I surrendered my life to God's call to the ministry: to be a missionary in Africa.

The night that I made my commitment to the ministry my first cousin, Dr. Arthur Walker, now secretary of the Education Commission of the Southern Baptist Convention, was preaching. He had a great influence on my life as did another cousin, Gerod Cole who today is a pastor in Tuscaloosa, Alabama. (In fact, I have six first cousins who are Baptist ministers.)

My schooling was at Howard College, now Samford University, followed by a one-semester stint at Golden Gate Baptist Seminary when it was still in Berkeley, California, finally completing my B.D. (since changed to M.Div.) degree at Southwestern Baptist Theological Seminary in Ft. Worth, Texas, in July of 1959. I was one of those who crammed three years of seminary training into five. I held student pastorates for my last two years of college in Alabama, was an interim pastor while in California, and pastor of First Baptist Church at Crowley, Texas, for three and one-half years while in Southwestern Seminary.

---

[1] The original version of this odyssey was given as a talk to a group of scholars and Church leaders at the Second Greek Orthodox/Southern Baptist Dialogue held at the Cedarmore Baptist Assembly, Bagdad, Kentucky, May 25-27, 1981. The request by Bishop Maximos, one of the convenors of the dialogue, was that I tell my own personal experience in coming to Orthodoxy. Obviously, any other of our bishops would have a different personal story to tell. But I trust the main details of the events pertaining to our corporate experiences that resulted in the birth of the Evangelical Orthodox Church are faithfully recounted.

During seminary our oldest daughter contracted bulbar polio and was very critically ill, being placed in an iron lung for some time. In addition, the polio developed into encephalitis and it appeared that if she did live she would possibly have severe brain damage. One of the great miracles of that whole episode is that she came out of all of that with only a paralysis of the left arm and shoulder muscles. We had prayed that if the Lord spared her life, He would leave her with a good mind. He answered that prayer, and she went on to graduate from college magna cum laude.

The whole experience was a very trying one for my wife and me. It required that my wife drop out of seminary, which meant she could not finish the remaining ten hours of school work required by the Baptist Foreign Mission Board for us to be appointed as missionaries in Africa. So, to fulfull our missions calling, we did the next best thing and took a small mission church in Xenia, Ohio in 1960.

We saw that church grow from 65 enrolled in Sunday School to almost 550 enrolled three years later. However, the baptized membership of the church only reached between 175 and 200 during that time. We built buildings and worked vigorously during that three-year period. I remember hearing the story of the little old lady who said, "I'd like to join your church, but I'm not physically able," and I thought that surely applied to us.

While busy as a pastor I was at the same time chairman of evangelism for the Greater Dayton, Ohio Association of Baptist Churches and had a great burden for world evangelization. In fact, I was actively involved in a number of evangelization projects including taking a large group of pastors and laymen to the island of Haiti for an evangelistic program.

Before leaving the subject of the planting of that church in Xenia, Ohio, I might mention that the Lord also gave us an opportunity to constitute a Baptist Church in Leeds, Alabama, some years before we went to Ohio. In 1980, I was invited back to the Dayton Avenue Baptist Church in Xenia, Ohio to speak for their 20th anniversary, and two months later to the Valley View Baptist Church of Leeds, Alabama, to speak for their 25th anniversary. I have always considered it an honor and a privilege to have been used of the Lord in establishing and serving those two churches.

At the conclusion of three years with those wonderful people in Xenia, we felt the Lord was calling us either into a missionary or evangelistic ministry. We had made strong efforts for my wife to complete the ten hours of schooling she was lacking, but our efforts continued to be thwarted. On one occasion just three days before she was to enroll I was in a light plane crash that almost took my life. Then the next semester, just four days before she was to enroll, I had to take her to the hospital in the middle of the night for emergency surgery. At that point I told the Lord that I wouldn't make any more efforts and that if He wanted us in Africa He would have to do it of His own accord.

Though we had been very happy in the work of the church in Xenia, it was because of a deep passion for evangelism and missions that I was especially open to an event that changed the course of my life. A friend told me about an organization called Campus Crusade for Christ which was devoted to the evangelization of the world in this generation. After investigating it and meeting the man who was, at that time, the Big Ten Regional Director of Campus Crusade, Mr. Peter Gillquist*, and believing that the Lord was leading me into campus evangelism, I resigned the pastorate and joined the staff of Campus Crusade in 1963. For us it was a great step of faith and for two years I experienced some of the greatest joys of my life: talking to thousands of college students about Christ. But all along I felt uneasy about the fact that we were a "para-church" organization and that we were not truly doing what Christ commissioned His church to do, baptizing the disciples and bringing them into Holy Communion and church life.

After a while I was "promoted up the ladder" and became increasingly disturbed over my inner conflicts concerning the issues of Scripture and Church life. During this time I did, however, become Coordinator of African Affairs and was given the opportunity of going to the continent of Africa twice and thus fulfilling a little bit of that desire to minister to Africans which had been implanted in my heart as a sixteen-year-old boy.

In 1968, I resigned from the staff of Campus Crusade. The burden to see the Church established as we see it in the New

_____
* Now the presiding Bishop of the Evangelical Orthodox Church.

Testament burned in my heart. But we had no leading from God to join any other religious or para-church organizations. Thus we were forced to rely entirely upon the Lord for our financial support. I promised my wife that if He did not supply our needs through the unsolicited gifts and support of friends, then I would find some kind of secular employment. We were continually amazed at how He so faithfully met all our needs, many times in nothing less than miraculous ways.

At that time, my wife and I and our four children (later we were to have a fifth child) moved to a farm near Mansfield, Ohio where we began, without really intending to do so, a ministry to the troubled young people of the late 1960's and early 1970's. With no advertisement whatsoever, young people began to appear at our door asking if they could stay with us for a period of time. Some of them stayed a few days and some a few weeks and some literally for a year or more. We found ourselves ministering to runaways, "Jesus Freaks", dope addicts of all kinds, as well as "straight" young people who wanted to deepen their commitment to Christ and learn something about Christian discipleship.

As a family we were still faithful in our attendance at the Southern Baptist Church nearby, but we could not succeed in getting the young people who were coming to our home and living there with us to attend our church. After some time had passed we had accumulated a number of young people who had made commitments to Christ and were trying to get their lives back together again. They began to ask me to hold services for them. My children joined in that request and finally I yielded to the pressure to do so.

We held these worship services in a large basement area in our home, and I'll never forget the first time we had communion there. I almost felt like lightning might strike since I had never had communion outside the four walls of a church building. Believing that the Bible taught that we were to have communion each Sunday, we instituted that practice and found it to be a very rich, blessed experience.

We saw many dramatic conversions and baptized many people within the first two years of our ministry at Grace Haven Farm. In fact, one night after a college and high school retreat I baptized 26 young people after 12 midnight in a spring-fed pond (which kept ice from forming) in a driving snow storm. As odd as that may seem to some, it was certainly a very powerful and memorable experience. Out of it many young students' lives were remarkably changed. Many gave up the use of drugs and became active members of Bible study groups in their schools.

To a lifelong Orthodox, it may seem the height of presumption for one who is outside the Church to baptize converts so freely. But for those of us in that position it seemed the logical outcome of our evangelism. Passages from the Bible such as Acts 8: 27 - 40, which describes the baptism of the Ethiopian eunuch by the deacon and evangelist Philip, seem to give full authority for doing so. Furthermore, something really happens in peoples' lives who experience this. It would be a mistake for Orthodox Christians to totally discount such experiences and to treat them as though they are not, in some mysterious way, a work of God.

Perhaps the answer lies in something I once heard Bishop Maximos (of the Greek Orthodox Diocese of Pittsburgh) say. "We in the Orthodox Church know where the Church is, but we do not know where it is not. This is a matter for God to judge, and it is entirely possible that the Lord has many sheep who are not in the fold as we know it."

Along with the experience at the farm, I was teaching a number of Bible studies in Columbus, Ohio as well as in other cities and towns in northeast Ohio. After a year and a half, the work grew increasingly intense and we were joined by a co-worker who had formerly been the vice-president of Campus Crusade. He and his wife and five daughters moved into a home next to ours and we labored together.

With all of this activity we still had no real church government or structure. We were into a "let the Spirit lead" kind of form. There was little or no discipline, and we were attempting to live as "simple brothers in pure grace." I must say that though there were many exciting things happening, the overall experience was rather gruesome. The lack of discipline and structure was almost impossible to live with.

In 1972, feeling that there was perhaps one leader too many at the farm and having an opportunity to begin a similar ministry in Nashville, Tennessee, my wife and I pulled up stakes again and with our family moved to Nashville to begin all over again. We took with us three single young people and, of course, our own family. On our first Sunday in Tennessee, since we knew of no church that we might attend, we held communion in our living room. The next week some friends wanted to know where we had worshipped and we told them. They asked if they could join us the following Sunday. So again, we had this informal kind of church experience going on in our living room.

In addition, I was teaching a number of Bible studies around the city in various homes, and these grew and prospered. However, the informal home church did not do well; perhaps because we were too unstructured and certainly too unsophisticated for the Nashville people.

In 1973, I met with a group of ex-Campus Crusade staff members in Dallas, Texas. Out of that meeting of about 70 people came a group of men who continued to meet every three months for theological study and to seek the Lord's guidance in the development of various works and churches which we had started since leaving the staff of Campus Crusade. After we had had about three of these quarterly meetings, the leadership of the group settled down to seven men, all of whom had been very closely associated as fellow-workers in Campus Crusade.

As we sought the Lord's guidance about the kind of churches that we were developing, we went back to the ancient Fathers of the Church to see what they did in those years just after the New Testament era. One of our men, Bishop Jack N. Sparks, put out an excellent edition of *The Apostolic Fathers* which was published by the Thomas Nelson Publishing Company. That caused us to study the Fathers much more carefully and it was the reading of St. Ignatius that completely changed my whole view of ecclesiology.

Realizing that he was the third bishop of Antioch, and that he served from about 67 A.D. to 107 A.D., and reading his description of the bishops and presbyters and deacons of his time was revolutionary to me. Also, his view of the Eucharist was exciting, but troubling. We began to see that the hermeneutic which had rejected bishops and sacraments as a later aberration of Church history was not on solid historical ground.

As this group of men continued to study and debate, we finally got to St. Athanasius and the Ecumenical Councils. If anyone could be credited with our conversion to Orthodoxy it would have to be St. Athanasius and St. Ignatius. These men have become great heroes of ours along with many others of the ancient Church.

But this did not come without many struggles. As we taught these things to our people, they reacted quite strongly and some were convinced we were headed in the wrong direction. Thus, quite a number left us and have since become outspoken critics. I'm sure we have made numerous blunders in our struggles to assimilate what we were learning. Our efforts to restore the commitment and discipline we saw in the Apostolic Constitution and other ancient Church documents were often misunderstood by others and undoubtedly poorly carried out by us. But our commitment to our growing understanding of Orthodoxy and to the catholicity of the Church drove us to continue on, no matter what the cost.

In the mid 1970's we formed the New Covenant Apostolic Order (N.C.A.O.) and the number of workers involved in planting and developing churches grew to about twenty men. At that time we had churches in the Midwest, the East, the South, the West, the Northeast, Canada, and Alaska. In reality, we took twenty or more denominations and made them into one. Sadly though, in 1978 my former co-worker from our ministry in Ohio chose not to continue with us on this path toward Orthodoxy and left. In doing so he took with him the churches in Ohio and the East. The sorrow and acrimony resulting from the separation have been difficult to live with. But we have now become officially reconciled with the help and mediation of mutual friends. It is a joy to be able to share friendship and fellowship again, although we are not united in our work.

During this period, in the early 1970's, we experienced what some of us believed to be a supernatural word from God which defined our vision and calling for us. A passage which the Holy Spirit had shown me in a time of deep distress and confusion as I was seeking guidance for my own life and ministry was examined in light of the way we felt God was leading us as a group. It was Isaiah 58:1-12.

Verse 12, which I had not been able to understand before, seemed to be the word especially given to the leaders of the N.C.A.O.: "Those from among you shall build the old waste places; you shall raise up the foundations of many generations;

and you shall be called the Repairer of the Breach, the Restorer of Streets to Dwell In."

We saw the "foundations of many generations" to be the Biblical foundations of the Christian faith as interpreted through the ancient Creeds and conciliar formulations of the Orthodox Church. We became convinced that of all the expressions of Christendom, Orthodoxy had most faithfully preserved the foundations of the City of God. But through the centuries heretics, like bandits and marauders, had ravaged and pillaged the City — the Church. Thus it is no longer safe for the people of God to walk her streets unprotected by a shepherd. There are still wolves and demonic beasts and zealous, though benighted, men seeking to proselytize and divide and destroy the flock of God.

We believe God supernaturally called us to give our lives and talents to "build the old waste places . . . and raise up the foundations of many generations". We would count ourselves blessed if it could be said of us; "you shall be called the Repairer of the Breach, the Restorer of Streets to Dwell In." If it appears to you that our perception of our vision and calling is grandiose or that we are suffering from delusions of grandeur, I beg of you to pray for us. We do *not* wish to think more highly of ourselves than we ought to think (Romans 12:3). On the other hand, we do not wish to be unfaithful to God if He indeed has commissioned us for this work.

By February of 1979 we had grown into a very close-knit and highly committed body of workers and churches. We knew that the Lord was leading us to take another step toward unity with Orthodox bodies in the United States and we felt that the best way to do that was to declare ourselves to be a denomination or jurisdiction of Orthodox Churches.

In doing this, we did a very uncanonical thing, though we were not aware of *how* uncanonical it was at the time. We were already functioning as Bishops on the Ignatian model in our churches, so the six of us (out of the original seven) who founded the movement secured a liturgy for the consecration of Bishops, formed a circle, and consecrated one another. Then we went to our first official council and consecrated thirteen other men. That day, February 15, 1979, the Evangelical Orthodox Church was officially born.

We have continued to grow in numbers and spiritual strength. Our churches are close-knit communities of love and service. And though a number of them have gone through periods of intense struggle in our journey toward Orthodoxy, they have, for the most part, continued to grow and prosper. We have developed a strong catechetical procedure and have, by means of a steady progress, entered into Orthodox theology and worship.

With this, the Eucharist has become the center of our life in Christ. By it we enter into the heavenly holy of holies week by week. Previously our emphasis had been primarily on mission and service. It's not that we have abandoned those two very important aspects of church life; we see them coming more and more into focus, but at the present time our emphasis is on a more correct and complete worship.

For those of us who came from a background of emphasis on mission and service, it has been a great change to make worship the center of our lives. From my own past the very word "Eucharist" evoked images of a dead Church bound by dead tradition and a theology of salvation by works instead of grace. I had no concept of grace actually flowing through the physical means of Baptism or the Eucharist. In fact, I was anti-sacramental, being certain that those who believed in sacramental theology denied the grace of God and Holy Scripture.

Not realizing it, I held a purely cerebral and rationalistic view of faith and grace. I perceived that primarily through the preaching of the Word of God (the Bible) God's grace was somehow beamed into our hearts and lives. Thus, my soteriology* depended entirely on a person's I.Q. If he didn't have the intellectual capacity to understand and believe, then his only hope (which I believed was assured) was that God's grace covered him anyway.

I believed that to be saved each Christian had to have a private conversion experience. And one should not be baptized until he could bear clear testimony to such an experience. In fact, I held that if one had not had such an experience, then any baptism prior to it was invalid. Thus, infant baptism was held to be invalid. One must wait until he reached "the age of accounta-

* *Doctrine of salvation.*

bility" (a totally non-Biblical term) to be saved. I sincerely believed my views conformed to Holy Scripture and I held no place in my thinking for Tradition, Creeds, or Councils. All these I believed to be dangerous additions to the pure and simple faith of the Bible.

To anyone who has read this far, and who is remotely familiar with Orthodoxy, it should be readily apparent what a tremendous trauma I was in store for once I began this odyssey. After seeing in the writings of Ignatius (A.D. 67 - 107) that the Apostles appointed bishops in every place and realizing the congregational polity was not indeed the Biblical polity, my theological dominoes began to fall.

Next, I and my colleagues faced the reality that Ignatius and all the earliest extra-Biblical writers held to a clearly sacramental and not symbolic view of what we had called "ordinances" but which the ancient Church called sacraments. The word "sacrament" comes from the Latin equivalent of the Greek word "mysterion" from whence we derive "mystery".

Our studies of the New Testament and all of the early Christian writings forced us to see what the truly Biblical view was, that in a mystery, grace *is* actually conferred in the sacraments. Now those verses that we had never underlined began to make sense! And a whole *new world* of grace began to open to us. Instead of losing grace we began to discover new dimensions of it. And furthermore, we found clearly that the ancients had developed a healthy synergism between grace and works instead of the unhealthy post-Reformation dichotomy between the two.

Then came liturgy! Surely it didn't matter what order of worship one followed as long as one believed the right things — or did it? The more we studied, the more we realized that the worship of the ancient Church was structured on two Jewish institutions, not just one as we had previously held. The Synaxis or public worship (Liturgy of the Catechumens) was modeled upon the Synagogue worship, but the Eucharist Liturgy (Holy Communion or the Lord's Supper) was modeled after the Temple worship.

Our studies brought us to see that there was liturgy in worship from the very beginning of church life. Then we saw it in the New Testament. In Acts 13:2 we find "As they ministered to the Lord and fasted . . ."; the word "ministered" is *leitourgia*

118

from which our word "liturgy" comes. It literally means "work of the people" but from the beginning has referred to the worship of the Church.

Then in Acts 3:1 and 10:9 we found the Apostles (Peter and John and Peter again) observing the Jewish hours of prayer. These were liturgical prayers prayed at the same hour each day and come from ancient Jewish practice. To this day the Orthodox Church uses basically the same Scriptures and prayers only with Christian adaptation and meanings included. Once we began to pray and worship liturgically we found a whole new dimension to the Christian life. There is something tremendously comforting and enriching to regularly use prayers and worship that have been used by the faithful for over 3,000 years! We found that liturgy isn't dead, it's people who are "dead" or "alive" to the Lord.

A careful study of early Church history revealed the essential role played by the Creeds. We first observed that there are several obviously creedal passages in the New Testament, such as I Timothy 3:16 or Ephesians 5:14. These passages were probably used in the early worship liturgy of the Church. Then as heresies continued to increase and plague the Church, the need grew especially for succinct Christological Creeds. Most likely the Apostles' Creed was prepared by the Apostles and it set the pattern for the later and essential Nicene Creed.

After all, only a few had portions of Scripture, and furthermore, those who had direct access to Scripture needed a proper hermeneutical standard by which to interpret Scripture. The modern rationalistic idea that anyone and everyone is qualified to interpret Scripture was never a part of the faith of the Ancient Church. Today we have every kind of heresy in the world claiming the New Testament for its authority. But all reject the ancient creeds of the Church.

Those who claim to have no creed but the Bible are less than honest. They inevitably look to a teacher or certain books or to the founders of their church to provide the principles by which they will interpret Scripture. Why not stick with those standards which were formulated by holy men of old and which have stood the test of time?

Perhaps our greatest struggles came in the area of the use of icons and the Orthodox doctrines concerning Mary. Concerning

the former we had been certain they represented serious violations of the commandment "Thou shalt make no graven images
. . . ." Was there not a danger of worshiping the icons? Some of us came from such iconoclastic backgrounds that we wouldn't even allow a cross to be worn or used in worship.

What we failed to see was the radical difference the Incarnation makes. Once God took on humanity it became possible, even essential, to use matter to depict the significance of that event. St. John of Damascus, in his very readable treatise *On the Divine Images,* excellently explains and defends the use of icons. But once we began to use icons in our worship services we needed no further defense. They have been a phenomenal aid to realizing we worship in the presence of the saints and heavenly hosts.

And as for the danger of worshiping the icon, I no more mistake it for the one it pictures than I mistake the pictures in my wallet for my loved ones. And St. John points out that the devotion expressed before the icon passes on to the prototype (the one pictured on the icon). But rather than debate the issue, the best argument is to experience the blessings the icons can be when they are properly used.

Regarding Mary, we did not wish to worship her or elevate her to the level of the Holy Trinity. I remember how I previously feared that was the case for those who honor Mary. But true Orthodox veneration of Mary is grounded in Scripture. Remember the declaration of Elizabeth, "But why is this granted to me, that the mother of my Lord should come to me?" (Luke 1:43). Indeed, the babe in Mary's womb was God from the moment of His conception. There never was a time when He wasn't God. And in order to be our Savior it was absolutely essential that the Second Person of the Godhead take upon Himself true humanity. Thus, Mary is rightly called "Theotokos" or "God-bearer". She was the mother of God. He joined Himself to her humanity for our sakes!

And just imagine the effects of having such an intimate relationship with the Son of God! It isn't possible to have God living within you without it changing you forever. The Church has held from earliest times that Mary was fully sanctified (deified) as a result of this relationship with Jesus.

Furthermore, she became the perfect example of what all Christians should be and do, one who completely and willingly receives Christ in both His natures, divine and human. We must emulate the Holy Virgin by coming in complete humility and obedience to Christ, receiving Him by faith into our hearts and lives.

This is what Orthodox Christians believe takes place in Baptism and the Eucharist. In Baptism we are joined into union with Christ. In the Eucharist we are nourished — every cell of our body and every part of our soul and spirit — by eating of His Body and Blood. We partake of His life in faith week by week as He Himself instructed us to in John 6:32 - 58. And without this sacrament we cannot effectively and consistently abide in Christ as every sincere Christian eagerly desires to do.*

Now back again to Mary: by inspiration of the Holy Spirit, St. Mary herself declared, "behold, henceforth all generations will call me blessed" (Luke 1:48). As I studied why the Ancient Church placed such a great emphasis on Mary it suddenly dawned on me that I had *not* faithfully "called her blessed." Rather, because of my anti-Catholic bias and because of my reaction to what I perceived to be an improper worship of Mary, I fear that I argued against venerating her and calling her blessed. I didn't see that the Church was saying that what Mary has become by sanctification/deification we *all* have the privilege of becoming.

We too should aspire to the holy standing which the Church declares the beloved Virgin has achieved: "more honorable than the cherubim and more glorious than the seraphim." As Hebrews, Chapter 2 indicates, we human beings presently occupy a place lower than the angels, but one day, through our union with Christ, we shall be exalted far above them. The Church holds that beloved Mary has already achieved that exalted state.

Obviously the theological milestones which we have passed have been revolutionary for us. I am aware that for many in the Evangelical world this does not represent progress but devolution. My only reply is that once one has tasted these blessed truths and the comfort they bring he loses his fear of them and begins to see why so many have fought and died for them throughout Church history.

---

* See John 6:56 and 15:1 - 12.

This is not to say I do not appreciate my heritage. On the contrary, I am grateful for my Baptist heritage and roots. From them I gained and never lost my deep love for the Bible as God's Word. It is still one of my greatest pleasures to preach and teach from the Scriptures in a verse-by-verse exegetical style. And of course I have come to love the commentaries of St. John Chrysostom in which I have spent many, many hundreds of hours, since he too followed the style of exegeting the Scriptures verse-by-verse and chapter-by-chapter.

Furthermore, for me the fervor and zeal for evangelism and missions comes by way of my Baptist heritage. In addition there has been planted in my heart a deep desire for genuine piety and holiness which I owe to my Baptist upbringing. Thus I feel a debt of gratitude to my parents and forebearers for all they gave me. I wish to go on record with all humility and sincerity in saying a warm "thank you"!

But I am also grateful beyond words for all that God has given us in Orthodoxy. From it we have received a greater love for history, for truth and theological accuracy, for richness of worship and the disciplines of dynamic spirituality, to mention a few things. Our association with godly Priests and Bishops has opened a whole new world of Christian fellowship and relationships for us.

Our Synod of Bishops was especially privileged to have Fr. Alexander Schmemann — of blessed memory — spend several days instructing us and challenging us in our journey. In addition, we have had Bishops Maximos, Anthony, and Dimitri, and Fr. Meyendorff and a number of others to come and encourage and enlighten us.

We humbly desire to be instruments used by Almighty God to "raise up the foundations of many generations" to "be called the Repairer of the Breach, the Restorer of Streets to dwell in."

Pray for us.

The Prodigal Son

by Father Tom Avramis

We are One in the Spirit,
we are One in the Lord.

The words of the song still ring in my ears as if it were just yesterday. The clapping of hands to the beat of Christian folk songs is still impressed upon my mind.

It was in the early 1970's and I had never heard of a group named Young Life until some friends invited me to go to a meeting with them. I was in high school then and having friends was priority number one. I had learned very early how important it was to surround myself with plenty of friends. It meant a great deal to be accepted and to have something to do with people you liked.

From the start of my Freshman year in high school I chose football as the vehicle I would use to gain popularity. It didn't matter that I was not a superstar; what was important was that I was on the team. My name would be on the roster and I would receive all the benefits that went with being a football player, one of which was the constant interaction with cheerleaders and songleaders. Seemingly trivial in retrospect, but how important at that time!

Through this interaction I grew close to several individuals who were involved in many of the same activities and were very well thought of. For several months they had been attending the weekly meetings of Young Life. I was invited to attend on several occasions but always managed to find excuses not to go. I was reluctant to do so, because a change had slowly occurred in their lives since they had been going to these meetings. When I finally attended a Young Life meeting, I found it rather harmless, as far as my social network was concerned; at first glance, anyway. It was an informal gathering where several songs were sung by fifty or sixty of us gathered on the floor of a "youth house". Following the singing, a few from the group spoke about what Christ meant to them. To end the meeting, the Young Life leader, a man in his mid-thirties, closed with a few words and a prayer.

I had mixed feelings about the whole affair, though, and it was not until a few days later that all of this sank in. The closeness and acceptance I felt there were extremely attractive, though the warmth did not seem to be based on anything I had done or who I was. It couldn't have been, since I knew hardly anyone there. At the same time, though, the religious nature of the gathering worried me. I knew that if allowed to grow it could threaten my reputation and the work I had put into building it. I couldn't afford to have the "religious" label hung on me. Yet, there was no mistaking the reality of this experience in the lives of my friends. This was the dilemma: to be threatened by something that was at the same time magnetic.

My experience up to those days, as far as religion was concerned, was purely Orthodox. I had known nothing else. For reasons I could not explain, I knew the Orthodox faith was the true faith. I was told this over and over again through the years in my Sunday School classes. Ours was the first Church and the only one which had remained true to the doctrines of the early Church. That's what I was taught and that's what I believed.

When I was six years old, I became an altar boy. Going to church became synonymous with serving in the altar, where I came to know others my own age. But in time, serving in the altar became a chore, and, to pass the time, we found a variety of interesting distractions to occupy us.

But if there was one thing I remember about my upbringing as an Orthodox, it was the commemorative nature of the worship: all we seemed to do was commemorate past events. My friends and the others at the Young Life meeting, though, spoke about Christ in terms of *now*. They spoke of the Christ experience as something more than a past historical event, speaking as though the Resurrection had just happened and we were the first Christians.

I don't mean to imply that my own family was not Christ-oriented. They were very much so, but the *meaning* of being Christ-oriented was not communicated to me by the Church. As a result, the tendency for faith to become merely a series of commemorations was strong.

What was good for my parents, however, was not good enough for me. What they could accept as truth without inquiry were the very things I questioned most. After all, my generation was the questioning generation. Vietnam was in full swing and the politics of the time were *the* issue. One of the side-effects of the Vietnam ordeal was the questioning of all authority, an attitude that can still be seen today. Indeed, this outlook, the calling to account, helped change attitudes in the United States, in many cases for the good.

Accordingly, it was not long before I leveled my anti-authoritarian guns at the Church and started to fire. The more I became involved in the Evangelical youth movement the more critical of the Church I became.

My base of reference was the Bible. Anything in the Church that could not stand the test of Biblical scrutiny was to be abandoned. The more involved I became in the Evangelical movement the more Bible I learned. The more Bible I learned the more volleys flew against the Church.

For example, icons were idolatrous and heretical. The Virgin Mary was not to be considered the "Mother of God" and "ever-virgin". She married Joseph and had several other children afterward. The saints, by the prayers they received from the Orthodox, were being given honor due only to God. The saints were emphasized to the detraction of Christ. Priests were called "Father" even though the Bible prohibited that title to anyone but God. The use of incense, vestments, memorial prayers for the dead, and other baggage in the Church also came in for scrutiny.

It was clear that my parish church was ill-equipped to withstand such an onslaught, especially from one of her previously loyal and active members. I was either dismissed as an adolescent undergoing a "search for self" who would soon come to his senses, or ignored altogether. It was not until my influence spread to other youth, who began attending Bible-oriented meetings with me and who began questioning the Church also, that parishioners realized something had to be done.

In time, the community was polarized: the sympathetic ones counselled patience and perseverance, while the hostile ones demanded action against us. We considered the priest at that time ineffective since he "did not know the Bible". His only recourse, which he took, was to turn to the bishop. When the bishop finally arrived in the community he was in no mood to deal with us. He was met by the same barrage everyone else had received. We demanded answers and insisted that *all* persons must have a "personal" encounter with Christ or else they will be damned.

Meanwhile, the sympathetic group hoped the bishop would provide us with answers to help us see the truth of the Church. The hostile faction looked to the bishop for strong and swift action to put an end to the confusion in the parish. But the bishop seemed not to be interested in our questions or what we wanted to know from him. Instead, he demanded that we straighten up or be excommunicated, a pledge he delivered angrily.

This crushed our families and at the same time elated the group that had urged severe and decisive action from the bishop. We rejoiced among the tears and smiles; after all, the Bible related to us that Jesus forewarned those who would follow Him that they would be rejected. We were overjoyed that we "had been considered worthy to suffer shame for His name" (Acts 5:41). Were it not for the personal intervention of my uncle, himself a priest, I have no doubt that the bishop would have made good on his threat.

Meanwhile, whether or not we were excommunicated was not one of our main concerns at that point. In fact, only our families were really alarmed by the possibility of excommunication, and inasmuch as we saw their pain, we tried to avoid further confrontations which might be highly visible and therefore risky.

My internal search for life vocation led me to believe that whatever I did must be full-time Christian work and would have to be directed toward, or at least involve in some way, outreach to the Greek community. After all, I was Greek and proud of that fact, and I wanted to share this experience of Jesus Christ with others of my race.

My activity in Evangelical circles did not abate. I was as active as ever. I also regularly attended the Greek Orthodox services, more for the sake of family harmony than for spiritual growth. I also used every opportunity to interject my Evangelical interpretation of the Bible into whatever situation I could. Constantly being in Orthodox situations provided me with plenty of opportunities to launch my customary attack against "unscriptural" Orthodox customs and traditions.

Tradition, I believed, was the root cause of all the other deviations in the Church. It stifled the Holy Spirit, not permitting God to operate and move freely in the Church. Tradition had replaced the Bible and subjected it to itself rather than vice versa. I saw little difference between customs and Tradition. I did not reject Tradition altogether; only where, in my view, it contradicted Scripture.

Tradition gave us the same liturgy every Sunday, over and over again. Tradition called for icons, prayers for the dead, prayers to saints. Tradition had us address priests as "father".

One of the features of Tradition that disturbed me most was the insistence that the Virgin Mary was "ever-virgin". I could accept that she conceived and gave birth to Christ as a virgin but not that she remained ever-virgin. After all, in Matthew 12:46-50 there is a reference to the "brothers and sisters" of Jesus. Furthermore, in Matthew 1:24-25, we are told that Joseph "kept her a virgin until she gave birth". I concluded, therefore, that according to the Bible Mary was not ever-virgin. The Evangelical position, as a matter of fact, is that Joseph and Mary had relations after the birth of Jesus and had other children.

But if this were true, where was Joseph at the Crucifixion? Why was he not with Mary at the foot of the Cross? And if she was indeed married to Joseph, why did Jesus give her over to the care of John instead of her own husband (John 19: 26-27)? The Evangelical answer, to which I subscribed, held that Joseph had died. But that is not Biblical, it is a tradition of sorts uniquely Evangelical. Why is there no mention of Joseph's death in Scripture? The death of Lazarus, a good friend of Jesus, is mentioned. Why no mention of His own father's death?

Then again, what about Joseph not knowing her "until" she gave birth, as in Matthew 1:24-25? As I inquired into the use of that word I found some interesting things. In Hebrews 1:13, the Father is quoted as saying to Jesus, "Sit at My right hand, until I make thine enemies a footstool for Thy feet". We find the word *until* used here. Following Evangelical logic, therefore, does this imply that Jesus will no longer sit at the right hand of the Father *after* His enemies are made His footstool? If we are to be consistent in our treatment of the word *until* the verses seem to say exactly that.

Another example is found in the account of Noah's Ark in Genesis. After the flood of forty days, Noah opened the window of the ark. According to Genesis 8:7, he "sent forth a raven; and it went to and fro until the waters were dried up from the earth". Does this mean that the raven never flew again after the waters were dried up from the earth? We would have to make such an assumption if we were to treat *until* consistent with Evangelical logic. Therefore, Joseph did not necessarily have relations with Mary based on Matthew 1:24 - 25.

As a final discovery, I found that in the year 431 A.D. the Third Ecumenical Council of the Church referred to Mary as "ever-virgin". This Council was convened hundreds of years before the Great Schism took place, and over one thousand years before the Protestant Reformation. What transpired at this Council happened long before Christianity became fragmented into various churches. Yet these early Christians, totally united in faith, refer to Mary as ever-virgin. All along, however, I felt that these positions of the Orthodox were not Biblical.

I was not alone in my thinking, for in my circle of Evangelical activity I had plenty of "brothers and sisters" who were only too eager to provide me with ample ammunition to use against the Orthodox who were "just like Catholics" anyway. What I was to learn later was that the term "brothers and sisters" can also be used to denote first cousins, and that the Orthodox Church taught that Joseph married another person and that the "brothers and sisters" were His first cousins. This comes to us through the Tradition of the Church.

Furthermore, the Lord Himself warned about the danger of tradition in Mark 7:8. St. Paul also stressed the pitfalls of tradition in Colossians 2:8. The very thing Jesus and Paul warned against I felt was happening in the Church. What I failed to see was the drastic difference between "the tradition of men" and the Tradition of God. For while I enjoyed quoting the above verses to my Orthodox friends, I totally ignored St. Paul's admonition to the Thessalonians to "hold to the traditions which you were taught, whether by *word of mouth* or by letter from us" (II Thess. 2:15).

Instead of making a distinction between the two types of tradition mentioned in the Bible, I lumped any form of tradition into the same useless category, a move which was clearly unscriptural.

On one occasion a priest I met had the willingness to go head-on with me on this topic. I came out the loser, or the winner, I should say, since it ultimately changed my thinking about Tradition and set me on the road back to the Church.

As I stood quoting my usual list of verses on Tradition with Bible in hand, this priest simply asked me how I got my Bible. Not knowing what he meant, I passed off his question lightly. He insisted on an answer to the question. Having never been challenged on such a basic point, I was caught completely off-guard and was without an answer.

He proceeded to explain to me that the same Bible I was so fond of quoting and venerating was itself part of the Tradition. I was appalled: the Bible part of a Tradition? But he pointed out that Paul speaks of oral and written tradition in II Thessalonians 2:15. The written Tradition he described as "letter" and, as we know, the majority of the New Testament letters were written by Paul. The Bible, therefore, is written Tradition, since the meaning of tradition refers to something handed down from generation to generation.

But what about oral tradition? Actually, he said, "the Bible was originally oral tradition until it was written down." Approximately fifteen years had elapsed between the Resurrection of Christ and the writing of the first New Testament book. Now here's the question: between Christ's Resurrection and the writing of the last New Testament book approximately seventy years had elapsed. What did the early Church do prior to the New Testament? We know for a fact that the early Church was alive and very active, yet the Christians had no Scriptures apart from the Old Testament and furthermore did not know that they would someday even have a so-called "New Testament".

Members of the early Church began meeting regularly to learn more about Christ and to follow the instructions He had given while on earth. Even St. Paul makes use of oral tradition in I Corinthians 11:23 - 30, where he quotes Jesus's words at the Last Supper *word for word*. But Paul was not at the Last Supper. How was he taught it? Oral tradition. What was unique about

Paul was his ability to make oral tradition become written tradition as well, the above verses being such an example.

Another strong support of Tradition comes from the last verse (21: 25) of the Gospel of John: "And there are also many other things which Jesus did, which if they were written in detail, I suppose that even the world itself would not contain the books which were written." This leads us to a rather interesting question: are the works and words of Jesus for whatever reason not included in the Bible any less than those that are included? The more I pondered such questions the more searching I had to do. For the first time a priest was able to throw back all that I was throwing at him. I was rattled and knew I would have to get to the bottom of this Tradition business. If there was indeed a "Tradition of God" I didn't want to miss it.

I started by looking at the Church as an institution. I say institution precisely because the word itself denotes something that was instituted for a purpose. Until my inquiry began into the origins of the Church I had always looked upon the Bible as an institution, but not the Church. What I found was shocking and completely opposite of all my previous thoughts. My focus was intended to be on the Church versus the Bible as God's authority on earth.

My first finding was this: Christ came to establish the Church, not the Bible, to carry on His mission. Time and again I saw the Church being referred to in the New Testament as Christ's body, His people, etc. Not once did I find a reference to Christ ever having spoken of a future book which would be the ultimate authority in Christian matters. Not once did I ever find a reference where any of the Apostles ever felt that way, either. Christ shed His blood for His people, His church, not a book.

In Matthew 16: 18, the Lord says "I will build my church; and the gates of hell shall not overpower it." As much as my Evangelical friends would have liked to substitute the word "Book" for "Church" in the above verse, it could not be done.

Later, in Matthew 18: 15 - 17, Jesus, suggesting how to handle a sinful brother, commands as final recourse that the sinful one be taken before the Church for judgment. There is no mention of a New Testament. In one of the most potent testimonies of the place of the Church, Paul (I Timothy 3:15) refers to the Church as "the pillar and support of the truth." He does not mention any kind of book.

My regard for the Bible was not affected at all by these discoveries. I continued, and still continue, to maintain that the Bible is the infallible Word of God. What did change, though, was my understanding of the place of the Bible within the Church.

The more I read and studied, the more I saw how it was the Church that in time decided to compile a canon which would eventually become known as the New Testament. The Church decided what would be Scripture and what would not. Many works never made it into the New Testament: the Church made those decisions.

Even though the individual books of the New Testament were completed within seventy to a hundred years after Christ, an official canon would take a couple of hundred years to develop. In the meantime, the Church was thriving without it. When the Church finally developed the New Testament canon it did not suddenly subjugate itself to it and pay homage to it as the sole basis of authority. On the contrary, the Church saw the canon as a complement to everything the Christians already had, which by then was substantial. Therefore, it was required that the New Testament conform to the Church and not vice versa.

Earlier I mentioned that I had considered, and still do consider, the Bible to be the infallible Word of God. Today all around us we see preachers proclaiming the same thing: that the Bible is God's infallible Word. Once, while proclaiming the same thing myself, an Orthodox Christian asked me if I was infallible. "Of course not," I replied. "Then," said he, "how can you possibly attempt to translate an infallible instrument while you yourself admit that you are fallible?" That one encounter did more to change my thinking about the Bible than any other I've had.

Since then I've come to see that an infallible instrument can only be interpreted by an equally infallible instrument like the Church. According to the teachings of the Orthodox Church, no one person can be infallible for "all have sinned and fall short of the glory of God," (Romans 3: 23).

However, the *Church* is infallible and can therefore in-terpret the Bible infallibly. If the Church is composed of all who are members of the Body of Christ and who as individuals are sinners, how can they collectively be infallible? Because when these individual sinners, who collectively make up the Body of Christ, gather as the Church, Christ is the head. The Church is infallible only because Christ is infallible. Ephesians 5: 23 leaves no question as to who is the head of the Church. Christ is.

This is why the Bible is so important. For the Bible was compiled by the Church with Christ as the head. Yet these same individuals also believed and taught other important truths as members of the Body of Christ. How could I, for example, easily accept the decision of the early Church concerning the New Testament and yet totally reject the teaching of these same Church Fathers on, say, the Eucharist.

My Evangelical exposure also led me to view the Eucharist as a memorial and not as the body and blood of Jesus Christ. Yet, as I read more about the early Church, I saw how the early Christians viewed the Eucharist as the body and blood of the Lord in reality.

How could I trust the judgment of the Church Fathers concerning the New Testament and reject their judgment in other key areas? What if they were wrong concerning the New Testament and right about other things? The mentality of being able to pick and choose whatever one finds palatable about the decisions of the early Church makes one a prime target of the Devil.

Once at a Young Life gathering at someone's home we decided to have a communion service. Grape juice and crackers (not very Biblical!) were distributed to all. The remaining grape juice was poured down the drain of a nearby sink. An Orthodox friend who came with me and I were astonished. "How can you just pour what's left down the drain?" my friend asked. "After all, we just remembered the sacrifice of Christ and used that grape juice as a symbol of His blood." At that point, all of the others present, none of whom were Orthodox, nodded in agreement. For the first time they were probably confronted by the idea that certain material elements are to be considered holy because of what they are used for. Even though spiritually we two Orthodox were far removed from the Church, we apparently retained certain concepts, in this case, the sacred aspect of Holy Communion. This also played a prominent part in my returning to the Church.

This experience with Holy Communion sent me to my Bible to discover the true meaning of the Eucharist. I wanted to believe that it was really the body and blood of Christ because the implications of such a truth would be spiritually revolutionary. My Evangelical bias, however, would not allow me to accept what was not Biblical.

In John, chapter six, Jesus referred to His flesh and blood as "true food and true drink." In Greek, the word *true* means the reality, or genuine. Furthermore, did He not say "this *is* my body . . . this *is* my blood" at the Last Supper?

Soon after, a priest introduced me to a book entitled *The Apostolic Fathers*, which turned out was not about the Apostles but about those who became the Church leaders immediately following the Apostles: those whom the Apostles specifically trained to assume the leadership of the Church. I had never known that such a work existed and was fascinated.

But it made sense. After all, if the Apostles wrote epistles, or letters, to the churches under their leadership, why wouldn't the next generation of leaders do the same? Even though their letters were not in the New Testament, they were still valuable historically. In fact, church leaders still issue messages to their churches; we call them encyclicals.

The one Apostolic Father who fascinated me was Ignatius of Antioch, who became the second bishop of Antioch around 69 A.D. Since Paul was not martyred until sometime between 64 and 67 A.D., Ignatius was definitely in the mainstream of New Testament activity, especially since he is thought to have been a disciple of the Apostle John.

Ignatius wrote several epistles as the bishop of Antioch. What I found challenging was that, in his letter to the Smyrnaeans (chapter 3), he warns them to stay away from those who deny that the Eucharist is the body and blood of Jesus Christ.

In several other letters he refers to the reality of the Eucharist, as well: Trallians, 2:8, Romans, 7:2, and Philadelphians, 2:4. Now here was a Church authority who, since he remained bishop of Antioch until martyred under the Emperor Trajan between 98 and 117 A.D., must have been accurate in his teachings. Surely, he would have been removed from office if he were guilty of heresy. But where did Ignatius get his view of the Eucharist? From the Apostles! He was taught and trained by them.

The more I realized how important it was to see the wisdom in the Church that Christ established, the more I saw how dangerous (and naive) individual interpretations of the Bible could be. I soon came to see how a thousand individuals could interpret the Bible however they wished, while claiming to be led by the Holy Spirit, yet disagreeing with each other, and having their own churches.

I soon began to see that I was becoming just one more voice claiming to be led by the Holy Spirit in my interpretation of Scripture. Who was I, anyway? Did I really think God would give me an answer much different from those of the early Christians and that I would be the one correct? Was I so spiritually arrogant? Apparently I was. How beautiful God's concept of the Church started to look!

But there was still so much I did not understand. At least, however, I was learning to give the Church the benefit of the doubt with her two thousand year jump on me. That was a big step for me—to submit and be obedient to the Church. When I finally did do so, it is amazing how much I was able to grow spiritually in my knowledge. Since then I have seen the refusal to submit and be obedient to the Church, with Christ as head, as the main impediment to understanding spiritual things *correctly.*

In time I saw how so much of what I used to believe was not even an issue until after the Reformation in the Western Church, scarcely four hundred years ago. Where was the teaching that the Bible is the sole source of authority prior to the Reformation? I do not find it. Where before the Reformation is the concept of instant salvation? Nowhere. Where prior to Luther is the notion of individual enlightenment being paramount as opposed to the collective experience of all God's people in the Church, existing under Christ as head? Non-existent. Where is the teaching that all who believe in Christ, regardless of the faith they profess, are members of His body, as contrasted to *The Church* founded by the Lord so many hundreds of years before these various faiths even existed?

After I had become a priest, a man walked into my office to challenge the Church's teaching on the divinity of Christ,

134

which he claimed was unscriptural. I explained to him that I had plenty of scriptures to prove my point and that I was sure he could also produce several scriptures to seemingly prove his position. "But," I said, "if you really want to get to the bottom of this let's go about this a little differently." He looked at me rather suspiciously as he nodded his head in tacit approval.

"I am going to prove to you that my Church has consistently taught the divinity of Christ from the present all the way back to the time of the Apostles and I will ask you to do the same." He looked at me with a puzzled look and asked, "What's that going to prove?" I explained to him how it would prove that one of us is wrong and one right. "If your church is Apostolic, which you claim, it is not too much to ask you to prove it," I said. I could account for every year of my Church's history from the time of Christ until now. "In fact," I explained, "I can show you the proceedings of my Church's councils where theology is clarified in the early years of Christianity. Certainly you can do the same if the historicity of your church is to be taken seriously."

"Well," he said, "we do have conferences annually, but we only started keeping records in the late 19th century. But I don't see why that is so important to you."

"Because Christ made two significant promises prior to His earthly departure:

1. That He would establish His Church and the gates of hell would not overcome it (Matthew 16:18). This indicates that there would be a starting point to the Church and that it will always exist.

2. That when the Holy Spirit is bestowed the fullness of truth will be in the Church (John 16: 13). There will be no need for a restoration or a re-establishment. The Church that Christ said He would establish would last forever and contain the *entire* truth about God. There would be no need to supplement this truth with anything else: it was to be complete, lacking nothing.

"Therefore," I concluded, "it is essential to show both the historic and apostolic nature of what you declare so that I may be sure that it is from God and not the result of any man's interpretation or any group's formulation. I am prepared to do exactly that with what my Church teaches. I await the same from you."

135

In time, that man left the group he had joined and united himself with the Apostolic Church of Christ.

The sad fact is that our Evangelical friends will never experience unity if they fail to come to terms with what the Church really is. In my own experience in the Evangelical movement, I was never able to put my finger on what the Church was really all about, largely because the Evangelicals themselves have for so long stressed the individual and his personal relationship with God. This has effectively relegated the concept of the Church to a secondary position, contrary to the wealth of lip service paid to it. As long as each local church is seen as "accountable only to Christ", what Christ Himself established as His church will not be realized.

Fr. Dimitri Staniloa, the Romanian Orthodox theologian, has correctly pointed out that the Protestants, for all their talk of the Pope, have themselves established their own, "paper pope".

My concept of the Church was drastically affected as I realized that the Bible was not the Church and the Church was not the Bible. When I came to see how the Bible was a part of the great testimonies and witnesses that form a large portion of the Church, my spiritual life was revolutionized.

Yes, God's grace was transmitted through His word. But it also flowed through the Divine Liturgy, the sacraments, the hymnology (which are packed with Scripture), the icons, and the host of many other treasures found in the Church. Even the Bible made much more sense as I read it without the necessity to interpret it. I no longer prayed and studied for the correct interpretations; I merely sought to know what the Church taught and interpreted concerning any given passages. After all, these things had been given to the Church by God long before I was ever on the scene and the Lord wasn't about to give me a different understanding than He had already provided to the Church. I started to take my first step back: obedience.

Earlier I mentioned how I was sure that I must pursue a full-time Christian vocation. As I slowly moved back to spiritual unity with the Church, this desire still remained within me. Though I started to contemplate the priesthood, those around me felt that I was still too "Evangelical".

Yet, of all the areas of Evangelical thought I was exposed to, one feature of my past that I have dearly guarded and fostered was my conviction that we Orthodox had to be much more Evangelical toward the world in general and other churches in particular. For, at the root of our faith, we are called to be Evangelical in spreading our message: the Orthodox message. It is for this quality that I would always be indebted to the Evangelical movement, not to mention how I grasped the importance and necessity of knowing Scripture, something we Orthodox have neglected far too long. After all, we put the Book together. *We* should know what it says.

As I spiritually grew more in Orthodoxy, I found myself drifting further away from my Evangelical friends and activities. Even though I had grown closer to the Orthodox faith I continued in my leadership position with Campus Crusade for Christ at the University of Arizona, where I was a student. I was in charge of an Action Group (Bible Study), I taught in the weekly Leadership Training Class, and frequently was the emcee at the weekly College Life gathering.

I was originally attracted to Campus Crusade because of its Evangelical outreach and nondenominational character. Nondenominational is normally meant to designate those organizations with no affinity to any church. During my time with Campus Crusade, and while I was discovering my true spiritual home, I had several opportunities to share with my Evangelical friends my reflections about the Orthodox Church. Remember, Evangelicals are taught that there is no "true church" on the earth, but that all who believe in Christ, whatever and wherever they are, make up the "church".

Many, who could not understand how someone who "knew the Lord" could go to a church that was like the Catholic Church instead of a "Bible-believing" fellowship, were dismayed, despite the fact that this was supposed to be a "non-denominational" group. Others were interested, and a few wanted to know more. Eventually, a few actually became Orthodox, one going on to become a priest.

The more I delved into my Orthodox faith, the more tension I felt between my Church and Evangelical thought. One small example: when a person, through Campus Crusade, gave his life to Christ, he was encouraged to associate himself with a local church. But this was just a noble sentiment. Many members of the Campus Crusade encouraged new believers to attend church with them. But nearly all were members of Protestant or Evangelical "non-denominational" churches. God forbid that I would invite them to my church, a "non-Bible-believing" church. When I did, however, tension was caused within the "Crusade" ranks.

Officially, nothing could be done since the organization prided itself in being "non-denominational". Practically speaking, the term "non-denominational" usually meant everything was acceptable as long as one steered clear of Orthodox, Catholic, and other non-biblically based churches. I was tolerated but still functioned in my usual capacity. I began to see, however, that Campus Crusade, this non-denominational organization, was teaching some very denominational doctrines, as do all "non-denominational" groups or churches. Although various churches teach that it is necessary to be "born again" i.e. to have a personal experience of Christ, there are serious differences as to how and when this occurs. But Campus Crusade has its own definite doctrine as to how and when this is supposed to happen. This teaching aligns them with only a minority of churches which profess the same view. Is this being non-denominational?

On one of my several trips to Campus Crusade headquarters in Arrowhead Springs, California, I was given the opportunity to join the staff, which for a time I seriously considered. I was given a package of materials to peruse and told I would have to sign the enclosed "statement of faith". Among the items on the statement was the acknowledgement that the Bible is the infallible Word of God and the only rule for faith and doctrine. I had to accept, moreover, the doctrine of the Trinity, a certain position on charismatic movements, and a negative approach to the issue of "speaking in tongues".

What problem could I possibly have with some of these items? Absolutely none! I believe in the Trinity, the Bible, etc. But what really hit me is that, for a group that claims no particular alignment to any church, they became very specific in what they thought others should believe, not only teaching that Christ is the answer and that people needed to know Him, but actually teaching what and how people should believe in Him. If that was not a church, then I didn't know what a church was. Yet, Campus Crusade insisted they were not a church, that they were there to assist churches. Apparently, they chose to assist only those churches that conformed to their definitions.

What in particular seemed to cause tension was my constant reminder to them of their brand of discrimination toward those not fitting their definitions. Yet, I remained until I had to remove myself when the prejudice became intolerable.

It started one evening at the Leadership Training Class with about seventy persons present. The head of the University of Arizona Campus Crusade for Christ chapter was speaking on the topic of interpreting the Bible. He cited various abuses that occurred because of misinterpretations of the Bible. The example he was about to use would be disastrous.

He had everyone turn to John, Chapter Six, where Jesus referred to His "body" and "blood" as being "true food and drink". At that point, I was hoping he was not headed where I thought he was headed. "Some people," he explained, "think that Jesus was referring to His actual body and blood in this chapter, and that Holy Communion is really His body and blood." I couldn't believe he was speaking this way, since several Orthodox and Catholic students in the "Crusade" were present. "It would be ridiculous," he continued, "to think that Jesus would actually expect people to eat His flesh and drink His blood, yet that is what a misinterpretation of Bible verses can lead to."

I left the room.

The next day I contacted him and told him we had to meet immediately. We met a few hours later and I expressed to him how out of place I felt his example was, seeing that several persons in attendance, who were Christians, had a deep respect for Holy Communion as the very body and blood of Jesus Christ. "By your comments," I explained, "you've made those of us who believe in the Eucharist appear as spiritual idiots who are deceived; yet we are also part of Campus Crusade."

He apologized and assured me that his slip was unintentional and that he did not wish to offend anyone present. I told him how, in a non-denominational setting, there was no room for that sort of thing to happen. He agreed.

"Now," I asked him, "how are you going to rectify the situation. You've made the Orthodox and Catholic students appear as sub-par Christians. I think it's important for everyone to

139

know that, among their own peers, many believe in the Eucharist as the real body and blood of Christ and yet are just as committed as anyone to the Lord."

"Well," he said, "I'll personally go to every Orthodox and Catholic student who was there and apologize."

I agreed with his solution, but felt it did not go far enough. "What about everyone else who heard it? What about a public retraction at the next meeting?"

That was out of the question. He personally thought that belief in the Eucharist as the real body and blood of Christ was unscriptural and saw no point in apologizing for that to students, many of whom felt the same. He would approach only those offended and that was it.

My position was that his comments were made publicly and must therefore be retracted publicly. Furthermore, a "non-denominational" organization should not allow such things to happen. By allowing such incidents to occur, the organization aligned itself with certain churches and against others.

I also challenged him to study the whole issue of the Eucharist from the early Church until the present and see for himself how the teaching on the Eucharist was only seriously questioned within the last several hundred years. I told him that I could prove to him that the Church had never *not taught* that truth.

He was set in his ways and would not change his mind. But neither would I. It was just too important. After all, we were not discussing incense or icons: we were dealing with the very core of an Orthodox Christian's spirituality: the Eucharist.

After several years of active participation, I withdrew myself from the Campus Crusade for Christ organization. I was thankful for the good it did me, but felt sorry for a group that failed to operate by the ideals and standards it set for itself. Today, I see Campus Crusade as nothing more than one of the several various Evangelical churches in existence but without the maturity to admit it. They are a church without authority, preaching but unable to baptize.

After graduating from the University of Arizona in 1977, I entered the Master of Divinity program at Holy Cross in Brookline, Massachusetts. Totally obedient to the Lord, through the Church, I felt the inclination in my heart to seek the priesthood. A few years later, in July of 1981, after completing my program at Holy Cross, I was ordained into the priesthood of the Orthodox Church.

Since then, I find it incredible how many times in my priesthood I have called upon my personal background. I have met many Orthodox going through what I went through. What a relief they express when they find a priest who has actually passed through the same difficulties! In addition, I have been able to relate equally as well to non-Orthodox as they challenge or inquire about the Church, since I, too, was not Orthodox for a time. I can see how the hand of God guided me through those years and back home where I belong.

What brought me back?

An open heart. An open mind. Putting Jesus first in all things. The recognition that I did not know everything about Christianity.

In the end, however, it was not me at all. For it was the Lord who said: "You did not choose Me, but I chose you . . ." John 15: 16.

A Disciple of Jesus

by David Giffey

"At that time Jesus declared, 'I thank thee, Father, Lord of heaven and earth, that thou hast hidden these things from the wise and understanding and revealed them to babes . . ." (Matt 11: 25)

With the understanding of a babe I was accepted into Orthodoxy on a hot Texas morning in 1972. Five years later during a solitary pilgrimage which took me from Greece and Mount Athos through the Middle East to India, I made a note in my diary: "It is finally beginning to dawn in my mind that I am a disciple of Jesus."

Christianity and the Western world has long cherished neat and quick religious conversions. We have placed value on decisive action even on the subtle battlegrounds of our hearts and spirits. Our most famous example of conversion has been the Apostle Paul, whose life was changed forever in a moment on the road to Damascus. We justifiably admire the stories of saints whose lives followed Paul's pattern. Mary of Egypt was a prostitute before her instantaneous conversion. How blessed these saints were to so quickly be placed on a spiritual path from which they never deviated. Truly they were saints of God!

The story you are about to read is one of conversion to Orthodox Christianity. But you will find this story less auspicious and less dramatic than stories of the saints. It will be a story in which doubts and puzzles are examined for their meaning, and in which years pass spent in studies and practices.

The only constant in this story is the constancy of God's love and grace. As for myself, the path toward God (I say "toward" knowing that it is far from complete) is paved with countless failures, prolonged periods of ignorance and dullness, many remarkable and unexpected blessings, and a general feeling of faith and hope in God.

The youngest of four children, I was born into a Roman Catholic family. We lived a peaceful life on a small dairy farm in

Wisconsin. My father, a second generation German-American, converted to the Roman church when he married my Irish mother. They didn't talk about religion very much in my presence. My father was a sensitive man. I surmise that he tolerated the regularity and ritual of our family's worship, but was a bit disdainful of the clergy. My mother's devotion to her church was the product of generations of practice in her family.

The first six years of my schooling were spent in a one-room country school: one teacher for eight grades. It was a happy time. My first grade teacher, who later became a nun, made my introduction to school a delight. Given the huge workload placed on country school teachers, I had plenty of time to read and draw. We students were free to do what we wished if our work was done and our mouths were closed.

For seventh grade I was enrolled at Saint Mary's, a large parochial school in the city. While I was sad to part with my country classmates, I was excited at the prospect of a new school. The nuns who were my teachers for the next two years were kind and intelligent. At Saint Mary's I was meticulously trained to serve as an altar boy. I was thrilled to be able to kneel at the altar and recite the "confiteor" in Latin at mass, or to serve the archbishop during a confirmation ceremony.

In spite of the positive experience at Saint Mary's, I chose to attend the large public high school instead of the Catholic high school. That choice was my own. I made it because I wanted to come into contact with a widening variety of people. However, I continued to serve as an altar boy for the 6:45 A.M. Sunday Mass every other week right up to my graduation from high school in 1959.

Contact with religion during the formative years of my life was happy and interesting. In writing this I perceive that it may sound too idyllic to be true. But it seemed true then as it does now. I have often listened to other Catholics or former Catholics describe the guilts and fears they carry with them from their childhood experiences with "the Church". Such was not the case with me. My teachers left me with a trust in God's love and the need to return it.

My upbringing, of course, was insular. Not until many years later did I learn that there was a small, thriving Orthodox community in town. Comprised mainly of Greeks and Syrians who were my high school classmates, the Orthodox worshipped in a tiny church across the street from an imposing Catholic church which I visited often. I never knew they were there.

After high school my interest in the Church waned quickly. I moved from under the family roof to attend a state university twenty miles away. My new freedom coincided with major changes which the Roman Church was making. This was the time of Vatican II. I was puzzled by the abrupt change from Latin to English. I had studied Latin for two years in high school and understood it quite well. The Church's new approach seemed too casual . . . almost careless. The theological basis for the changes was never clearly explained to me. Add to this my personal desire for independence. For the next ten years or so I gave little thought to things having to do with church.

The highlights of my brief college career were extra-curricular. I became a John F. Kennedy zealot, an admirer of contemporary American literature and jazz. The elementary education courses I had chosen were unutterably boring. After a year, I dropped out to spend a year working and traveling from the East Coast to San Francisco via Mexico. Since that time travel has been my preferred classroom.

A chilling midwinter hitchhiking journey back to Wisconsin encouraged me to re-enroll in college. This time a friend and I were summarily punished for founding a student-operated literary magazine. The little periodical — there were only two issues printed — naively flew in the face of administrative control. That was my last experience as a college student.

Answering an ad for summer help at the local daily newspaper, I was given a spelling test and hired as wire editor. It was my job to select, edit, and lay-out the front page and all the stories reported from the wire services for a paper with a circulation of about 30,000. After one week of training I was turned loose in the wire room. One of my greatest difficulties was getting to work on time. It was an afternoon paper, which meant work began early in the morning. I was expected to open the building and have the wire copy sorted and sent to countless desks when the city room staff arrived at 7 A.M. At age 21, with an active social life to worry about, I frequently sprinted to the office from my apartment through the dawning streets of Oshkosh, Wisconsin.

Journalism in various forms occupied the next ten years of my life. The assassination of John F. Kennedy was demoralizing. I was moved to revisit California and spent a couple of months washing cars near the San Bernardino freeway. In March, 1964, I was drafted into the U.S. Army. My first year was spent at Fort Riley, Kansas, as a member of the 1st Infantry Division newspaper staff. In 1965 I was editor of the ship's newspaper as we sailed to Vietnam, where I remained as a combat photographer-reporter (propagandist) until my discharge in 1966.

A progression of newspaper jobs followed. I came to specialize in political writing. My stints gainfully employed by daily papers were interspersed with periods of civil rights journalism involving migrant farm workers who struggled to survive in Wisconsin. I worked as well with the anti-war movement. In 1969 I moved to the Rio Grande Valley of South Texas to edit and write (and type and deliver and all else) a Spanish-language newspaper for the United Farm Workers' Organizing Committee. After a year of exhausting work along the Mexican border, I sought refuge and recuperation in Austin, Texas, a pleasant city with a large community of people in sincere pursuit of a new age.

Employed to do odd jobs at *The Texas Observer,* a political periodical, I ended my career in journalism for the time being as a volunteer writer and cartoonist with the *Rag,* Austin's classic underground newspaper. Life as a journalist placed me in danger of a cynicism which I suspected was unhealthy and unproductive.

There followed a succession of construction jobs and day labor as I began to discover in myself a great wish to draw and paint. I let my hair grow nearly to my waist. I lived comfortably in the Mexican-American community in a pleasant rented house. To pay the rent I painted signs and billboards. I helped build a show ring for the Austrian royal Lippizaner horse show that passed through town. With a crew of Blacks, Chicanos, and long-haired Anglos I spent a summer pouring concrete basketball courts and picnic tables in the parks of Austin as part of a city recreation department program.

Those were valuable years. I was nearly thirty years old, an elder among my peers. I suffered not from a lack of ambition, but from a lack of certainty about what I should do. So I chose to do many things, and to be patient. My painting grew in importance. I made hundreds of canvases showing brightly colored fantasy landscapes with people and animals and birds playfully together. These I sold at a year-round street market.

An Orthodox theologian once successfully debated with a group of bishops and pointed out to them that the church formerly embraced by a convert to Orthodoxy probably existed in the grace of God since it had led the convert to Orthodoxy. The logic is indisputable. One wonders if we might not include other beliefs in general.

Many of my friends in Austin were deeply involved in the mystical religions of the Far East, specifically Hinduism and Buddhism. I was 29 years old when first I visited the church of the Prophet Elias in Austin. My hair was tied in a pony tail.

A handful of worshippers kindly tried not to stare at me. Most of them were Syrian-American. It was a church in the Antiochian Archdiocese. The semi-retired priest was tall, elderly, and a living example of God's greatest commandments. I knew none of these things. I had no knowledge of the multiplicity of Orthodox jurisdictions in the United States, or of the complicated intertwinings and overlappings between ethnic groups which brought their immigrant churches with them to America.

All I knew was that I felt at home. The Divine Liturgy touched me in ways the Latin mass had done for the first twenty years of my life. The fragrance of incense and the music awakened all my senses. A few people received Holy Communion. I wanted to but suspected correctly that I would not be allowed to do so.

By this time I too had become involved with Hinduism and meditation. That night as I sat cross-legged on the floor of the tiny room reserved for meditation at home, I spent some time staring at a picture of Jesus (a print of a Western style painting), which shared a low table with pictures of sages and saints from all over the world. They were there to inspire meditation. I was familiar with the amazing stories told of their lives. During the previous decade I neither denied nor embraced Christianity. My visit to the Syrian church had been inspired by the words of a Hindu swami, a spiritual teacher who knew much about Orthodox Christianity.

Each Sunday thereafter I showed up at the Syrian Orthodox church. I continued the practice of private meditation and hatha yoga in the little house which I shared with a small dog.

Life as an artist paid modestly. It kept me in art supplies and the necessities of life. Since I had earlier stopped eating meat or fish, my meals were inexpensive. Life was quiet. My friends were other artists, musicians, writers, political activists, and a host of converts to Buddhism or Hinduism. I became conscious of the wonders of Byzantine iconography and copied a painting of the Russian master, Andrei Rublev. It was the head of an angel, my first attempt at iconography.

Soon after the first visit to the Orthodox church I bought a copy of a small book called *The Way Of a Pilgrim*. It was the firsthand account by an anonymous Russian pilgrim of the spiritual path he had followed more than a hundred years ago. In his wanderings to learn the secret of success in spiritual life, the pilgrim was taught to practice the Jesus Prayer: "Lord Jesus Christ, have mercy on me." The practice of ceaseless prayer became a way of life for the Russian pilgrim.

So sweetly told was the story, and so inspiring were the results, that I immediately adopted the Jesus Prayer and attempted to repeat the prayer over and over during meditation.

The study and practice of Far Eastern religion continued, however. Within months, I was persuaded to move into a Hindu monastery. My head was shaved after the fashion of Hindu monks, and I spent six hours daily, three at dawn and three at dusk, in silent meditation, using the Jesus Prayer learned from the long-dead Russian pilgrim. But life there distressed me. Unwilling to submit to the rigorous monastic routine, I felt deprived of my freedom and independence. I couldn't watch the sunset if I wished to do so. I was distracted by the simultaneous practices taken from several religions which I found around me.

Less than three months later, I left the Hindu monastery taking with me little more than my bald head and the Jesus Prayer. I returned to Austin to retrieve my faithful dog. She had been a possession from whom I painfully parted at my "renouncing the world sale" when I entered the monastery. At the church of Saint Elias I was anointed with holy chrism by the Syrian priest, and was even invited to serve as an acolyte at the services.

By the grace of God I am a Christian man, by my actions a great sinner, and by calling a homeless wanderer of the humblest birth who roams

148

from place to place. My worldly goods are a knapsack with some dried bread in it on my back, and in my breast pocket a Bible. And that is all.[1]

" . . . a homeless wanderer . . . who roams from place to place" in 20th century America is variously called a hobo, a hippie, or a fugitive, but seldom a pilgrim. Yet the lessons learned by the Russian apply precisely to this story.

I moved back to Wisconsin, the state of my birth, where I found a home in an abandoned chicken coop on a peninsula of land which interrupts the northwestern shore of Lake Michigan. Don't worry: it was a nice chicken coop. And my presence there was by choice, unlike the migrant farm worker's family who were its last occupants.

I was lonely sometimes, especially during the long winter nights when my eyes tired early from reading by kerosene lamp light. I read a great deal of Orthodox literature old and new. Timothy Ware*, himself a convert, was a favorite. The early Fathers and explanations of the use of icons occupied time not spent painting pictures and cutting wood.

The peninsula called Door County, I realized years later, approximately resembles the shape of Mount Athos in Greece. But it was several hours by car to the nearest Orthodox church. After a year in the chicken coop I moved to a small farmhouse near Madison, Wisconsin where I was welcomed with remarkable affection and kindness by the priest, *presvytera,* and community of Assumption Greek Orthodox Church.

Something must be said about Father George. From my retrospective view, Father George's presence then and there was obvious proof of the existence of God. For five years Father George amplified the teachings of the Church through his patience, strength, and reluctance to judge quickly. He embodied the best in pastoral care. His manner was a practical teaching in love. Thank God for Father George.

As an artist, I struggled to learn iconography. Books from the library failed to reveal important steps in the ancient tech-

* *Now Bishop Kallistos.*

[1] *The Way of a Pilgrim* and *The Pilgrim Continues His Way,* translated from the Russian by R. M. French, Ballantine Books, New York, Second Printing; November, 1979, p. 1.

niques of Byzantine art. I visited Greece for the first time in 1977. For months I studied icons on church ceilings, walls, in roadside shrines and museums. My teachers were ancient paintings which spoke silently of the devotion of their painters. Through wonderful strokes of grace I met and observed some of the modern masters of church painting who answered my naive questions with good humor and honesty.

Then I caught the *caique* to the Holy Mount Athos. One hears many stories of the monks of Mount Athos. Those who speak ill of them generally do so from ignorance, misunderstanding, and fear. The monks of Mount Athos live in a time and place removed from the secular world. It is not surprising that these men whose victories are found in the achievements of the spirit should be judged harshly by a society grounded in matter.

For thirty-three days I lived in those amazing monasteries. The buildings were organic outcroppings of the mountains themselves. The monks I met were generous to a fault. The natural beauty of the countryside was unequalled. I sat for hours watching iconographers at work. I was told of the system of prayer and techniques required for making icons.

The spiritual father I met there gave me a new name, Philotheos. The name has become an addition to my conscience itself. How does one qualify as a "friend of God"?

The essential ingredient of the Holy Mount was prayer. "Prayer is like a turtle shell," a monk said. "We can hide under it when we are attacked by the devil." In the most spiritually active monasteries the monks conducted life against a backdrop of the Jesus Prayer. They prayed aloud at work in the gardens or silently with their prayer ropes in church. Conversational speech lost much of its meaning. As the way of life became familiar, I became an observer of spiritual warfare in myself and in those kindly blackrobed figures around me.

The human face reveals heartbreak, ecstasy, and all things in between. In the faces of some monks, apprentices at the world of discipline, there was to be seen sorrow and conflict. Others radiated an unaffected calm which was nearly palpable. Worship in the ancient and darkened churches was transporting: centuries of prayer paved a smooth path to meditation on God.

How one's perceptions changed! Tiny oil lamps which at first seemed silly and without purpose became beacons leading one to venerate the icons they scarcely illuminated. But what, I wondered, guided a blind monk along his daily path to kiss each icon in the church? Regarding the physical plane, the answer was obvious. The blind monk simply counted doorways and measured distances with his fingertips, and thus found each icon. But what was his inner vision? Icons are visual aids, are they not? They are made for the sighted faithful. Yet greater feeling for these painted images is seldom seen in those with useful eyes.

Here was a paradox of the highest order, an icon which served as a focal point for the inward-gazing veneration of a blind man. He venerated the icon not "in spite of" his blindness, but "because" of it. The blind monk kissing an icon seemed an incarnation of apophatic theology, the theology which leads to God by describing what God isn't, thereby tacitly and completely describing what God is: all else.

Not every monk was silent. Some delivered lengthy lectures to this blue-eyed foreigner. "Orthodoxy can be understood from a 'Protestant' viewpoint or from a 'Catholic' viewpoint," said one of them. "Orthodoxy must be accepted for itself if it is to be real. Orthodoxy is a godly way of life, and it is peculiarly Orthodox."

At first I was troubled by the paradoxes of life at Mount Athos. The monks reciting the Jesus prayer aloud seemed a distraction. Soon I too found it helpful to repeat the Prayer aloud until it captured a spot in my concentration. Then the Prayer could continue audible only to the inner hearing. The words were savored as sweet candy, each one rich and filled with love from and toward God.

The sign of the cross used by the Orthodox to bless themselves is a simple act endangered by human carelessness and repetition to lose its meaning. But I learned a new reality regarding even this simple gesture. The sign of the cross seemed as a wide furrow plowed around the heart, mind, and soul, and protecting them from the flames that destroy concentration in prayer.

After five weeks on the Holy Mount, my shoes were wearing thin from the rocky paths. I left. The world to which I returned seemed foreign and noisy.

From northern Greece I visited the Patriarchate in Istanbul, Turkey, where His Holiness Dimitrios gave his blessing. Within a month I was in India to explore the residue of years spent studying Oriental religions.

The God who made the world and everything in it, being Lord of heaven and earth, does not live in shrines made by man, nor is he served by human hands, as though he needed anything, since he himself gives to all men life and breath and everything. And he made from one every nation of men to live on all the face of the earth, and having determined allotted periods and the boundaries of their habitation, that they should seek God, in the hope that they might feel after him and find him.[2]

My path was narrowing, becoming less eclectic. The sages of Hindu and Buddhist India encouraged me to practice Orthodox Christianity. Their understanding of Christianity, of course, was Oriental. But their generosity of spirit did not make it impossible for them to appreciate a foreigner's feeling of his God. Some Indians tried even to include Jesus Christ in the pantheon of their worship as I had in my own way done years before.[3]

Occasionally Orthodox theologians make brief allusions to Oriental religious practices. The most common one is a comparison of the mantra, a phrase repeated during meditation in the Far East, with the Jesus Prayer, as formulated by the hesychasts of Orthodoxy and practiced widely among Orthodox people around the world. This comparison is wise and accurate to a point.

More common, however, is the blind denial of godliness and sanctity which many Christians hold for their Oriental brothers and sisters. I have found great relief in the understanding that spiritual achievements or failures elsewhere among peoples who practice other religions could never be a threat to my own practice of Orthodoxy. How could they be? Religious prac-

---

[2] Acts of the Apostles, 17:24 - 26.

[3] Please do not misunderstand or be scandalized by their attempts, fellow Christians. While their views of the reality of Jesus Christ may have been erroneous, they came nonetheless from love and devotion. To illustrate another side of the same coin, the Greek listeners at a lecture once delivered by a renowned Hindu sage who visited Athens politely filed forward to kiss the speaker's hand at the end of his talk. How could they have known that this respectful greeting normally reserved for Orthodox clergy would shock the sensibilities of many of the people of India where respect for another is shown by leaving them untouched? Other paradoxes were to be seen at that lecture. The speaker was barefoot, dressed in saffron-colored robes and sat on the floor. His listeners wore suits or dresses, shoes made of cowhide, and sat on folding chairs. The speaker's name, translated from Sanskrit, was the quotation: "Existence - Knowledge - Bliss."

tices and prayers seem intended to fill a personal storehouse from which can be withdrawn strength and understanding. Practice hopefully creates an intuition or reflex toward goodness in the practitioner which would override the base and sinful side of my nature. I need to rely on teachers for guidance, and not to second guess the activities of God. The voice heard by Saint Anthony the Great had spoken profoundly when it said: "Anthony, attend to Yourself; for these are the judgments of God, and it is not for you to know them."

I am now approaching the middle of my second decade as an Orthodox Christian. My work as an iconographer has demanded concentrated study regarding the Church. We converts by choice and by God's grace are lucky in many ways. To satisfy our curiosity we often read and ask questions which stem from our ignorance. We don't even know what is available to be taken for granted.

Over the years I have watched with fascination as my countless and dear Greek friends have accepted me as one of their own. Irksome at times to a prideful Irish-German-American, I have grown to understand as a historical accuracy what at first blush appears to be a case of mistaken identity. For example, in the old days, a person who converted to Judaism became a Jew regardless of ancestry. When I am told that, because of my work and travels to Greece, I am "as Greek as the Greeks", I now interpret it to mean a generic Greekness not confined to *foustanella* and *kourambiedes*.

While I share Christianity body and soul with Greeks, Serbs, Russians, Syrians, and many others, I cannot share in their nationality. I can love and admire it as an outsider, but my national pride is more excited when I hear the Clancy Brothers singing a song of the Irish Revolution, or recall the stories my father told of his father who ran off as a teenager to join the Union forces in the Civil War. Without the benefit of generations in the Orthodox church, I see little connection between one's bloodline and faith in God. The truths of Orthodoxy have never been in the keeping of a single ethnic group, for truth is universal.

During my first visit to Greece, I quickly found it necessary to begin learning the Greek language, which I find useful and interesting. My first phrase was: "I am Orthodox." My path into churches and to receive Holy Communion was often blocked by people justifiably protecting the sacred feast from the non-Orthodox. And they were always kind and interested upon learning that Orthodoxy could include fair-haired, blue-eyed Americans.

Years ago my initial response to Orthodoxy was awe. The awe remains, supplemented now with a deepening love for God and for those frequent instances when the Church illuminates for me the teachings of God. Increasingly, I "think" in terms of Orthodoxy much like an expatriated person might speak the new language but "think" in his mother tongue.

I love the Church for its sober dignity, for its intelligent theology, and for its gift of freedom, among other things. Errors, even crimes, committed in the name of Orthodoxy I abhor as any other. The pogroms of Imperial Russia, for example, in which Jews were massacred and their property destroyed sometimes coincided with feast days of the Orthodox Church. Dignitaries of the Church and civil officials shared responsibility for permitting or, in some cases, inciting such anti-Semitic brutality, which did not spare even Jewish children. They are the crime of humanity and misinterpreted teachings. That does not excuse them. God must (may) do that.

If the Orthodox Church were somehow embodied in a single human persona, I think she would weep with sorrow at the trials of all human life. To hear her name used to justify any act of vengeance or violence unworthy of God's children would utterly break her heart.

I said that I love the Church for its gift of freedom. Timothy Ware said it better: "True Orthodox fidelity to the past must always be a creative fidelity . . . . Tradition, while inwardly changeless (for God does not change) is constantly assuming new forms, which supplement the old without superceding them."[4]

My definition of conversion remains incomplete. What about the elderly monk who told me on Mount Athos: "I was brought back to God by Billy Graham." Is that monk a convert?

Lacking the lightning fast experience of Paul on the road to Damascus, I must describe my conversion to Orthodoxy as life itself. It is a setting against which decisions and choices of daily

---

[4] *The Orthodox Church*, Timothy Ware, Penguin books, 1972, 1973, p. 74.

life occur. Years after my initiation into the Church, I recognize that my conversion, if it occurred at that moment, was a sacramental spark which needed to burn more brightly. Had I been born into the Orthodox church, chances are I might have followed a very similar path, uniquely personal yet shaped by every teaching along the way. My conversion was not a single act in time. I can't place conversion in time because it continues to this moment. And I know that experiences like mine have been shared by others who were nominally Orthodox from birth. Are they converts, too?

Conversion has not been based on any strength of mine. The exact opposite is true. I have acted from a position of weakness in the hope that I would gain some guidance and strength. God has blessed me with life. He has given me every opportunity to seek and find him. He has even gone so far as to match me with a wife whose spiritual honesty and insights are exemplary of a true seeker.

But so much remains to be done. I sometimes feel as though I'm running a cross-country foot race with God. He is always the forerunner. When the race began I was excited and eager, always rushing to keep God in sight. For a long time now, in the middle of the race, the anxiety I feel at losing sight of God is replaced by a wordless certainty that I will continue to run.

God disappears over hills and behind trees. I need to rely on my desire and need and training to keep up, or just to stay in the race. As the race continues I am less obsessed with wondering at the whereabouts of God. I am reassured to know that he is still there, of course. Then the race course crosses a wide open field where I can comfortably watch God, and I settle into a steady pace. My mind is less self-centered. For a time I am not even conscious of myself. I have completely accepted my relationship to the leader of the race. I think about other people for a change. Then the anxiety pops back, and with it the fear of losing the race and other ego involvements. But gradually I become familiar with the new terrain and the other runners again. God knows this. He senses my lengthening times free from worrying about winning the race. He allows the gap between us to narrow. And then, in my imaginary foot race, at the perfect moment when I am miraculously free from little deceits and not even trying to catch the leader like a hunter after its prey, I round a corner of the path. There God is, stopped in his tracks, and I am enveloped in him. I am not surprised because the race has taught me to continue over obstacles. I am not concerned with the race at all, anymore. I am simply there with God, whether walking or running, living or dying. At that moment, if God wills that it happen as I imagine, my conversion will be completed.

When I came to the end of the things I had to tell, I said to my spiritual father: Forgive me, in God's name. I have already chattered too much. And the holy Fathers call even spiritual talk mere babble if it lasts too long. It is time I went to find my fellow-traveller to Jerusalem. Pray for me, a miserable sinner, that of his great mercy God may bless my journey.[5]

[5] *The Way of the Pilgrim*, p. 87.

Contributors' Biographies

AVRAMIS, REV. TOM. While at the University of Arizona, from which he was graduated in 1977 with a B.A. degree in Sociology, Father Tom was a campus leader and course instructor with the Campus Crusade for Christ. Four years later he received his Master of Divinity degree with Distinction from Holy Cross Seminary and was assigned to the Holy Trinity parish in Phoenix, Arizona as assistant priest. In 1983, after the sudden death of Fr. Michael Makredes, he was assigned to the Resurrection Church of Castro Valley, California, where he is at present. He is married to Alicia Lorraine Avramis, a convert from the Methodist Church. They have a daughter, Alethea Christina.

GIFFEY, DAVID. Though an iconographer now, Giffey has been a journalist in Texas and Wisconsin (1961 to 1971) and a combat photographer-reporter in Vietnam for the 1965-66 tour of duty. He has traveled to Mount Athos extensively, where he trained in the technique of Orthodox iconography. His works are exhibited in various galleries in Wisconsin, Minnesota, and Texas. Of his religious art, ceiling and wall paintings can be seen in the Churches of the Assumption in Madison, Wisconsin and of the Holy Unmercenaries in Rochester, Minnesota. Between 1977 and 1984 Giffey has executed approximately 150 portable icons for churches and individuals in the United States and several foreign countries. His *Life of Saint Kosmas* is in press.

KING, MARIA VALERIE. Associate Professor at the Medical College of Georgia in the School of Nursing in Augusta, Georgia. While a member of the Episcopal Church she belonged to the Order of Saint Helena, a monastic community for women, from 1959 to 1968, serving two years in Bolahun, Liberia, West Africa, as a nurse, teacher and evangelist. Since being received into the Greek Orthodox Church on the Feast of the Koimisis 1979, she has served on the Parish Council, the Stewardship Committee, written the weekly parish newsletter, and served as

Church Librarian. Currently Maria represents the Diocese of Atlanta on the Archdiocesan Board of Missions and is a doctoral student at the University of Georgia. She is a member of the Orthodox Church of the Holy Trinity in Augusta, Georgia.

McSHANE SUSAN. A licensed practical nurse with Mercy Hospital in Baltimore, Maryland, Susan was trained at Union Memorial's Johnston School of Practical Nursing, where she was graduated in 1977. She attends the Annunication Cathedral of Baltimore.

MORRIS, REV. JOHN W.. With academic preparation initially in German history, Father John Morris received his M.A. (1971) and PhD. (1974) from Oklahoma State University. Among his published works are *The Road to Olmutz: The Career of Joseph Maria von Radowitz* (1976), *Revisionist Historians and German War Guilt* (1977), *The Weimar Republic and Nazi Germany* (1982), and *The Charismatic Movement: An Orthodox Perspective* (1984). Father John, who has an MTS degree from Holy Cross Greek Orthodox School of Theology, was ordained to the priesthood on April 27, 1980 in Boston, Massachusetts by Archbishop Elia of the Greek Orthodox Patriarchate of Antioch. He is pastor of Holy Spirit Antiochian Orthodox Church in Huntington, West Virginia. He is married to Dr. Cheryl Haun Morris and has two children.

O'CALLAGHAN, FR. PAUL DESMOND. A native of Marin County, Fr. Paul received his degree in Religious Studies at California State University at Chico (1977) and Master of Divinity degree from Holy Cross Greek Orthodox Theological Seminary (1980). Was ordained to the priesthood of the Orthodox Church in 1979 by Metropolitan Philip, Primate of the Antiochian Orthodox Christian Archdiocese. He and his wife Jeannie are the parents of two children. Presently Pastor of St. George Antiochian Orthodox Church in San Diego, he has published *An Eastern Orthodox Response to Evangelical Claims* (1984).

SCOTT, FR. ANTHONY. Was born in Texas and grew up on Air Force bases in the southern and western sections of America. Paternal side of family originated in southern Germany and settled in upstate New York in the 1740's. Mother is half Hispanic and half German. Another branch of the family were among the first converts of Joseph Smith to Mormonism and on the original wagon train led by Brigham Young to Utah. B.A. University of California, Berkeley in 1971. Graduated from St. Vladimir's in 1975. Ordained to priesthood, 1974. He and his wife, a convert from Roman Catholicism, have three children. Father Anthony serves in one of the two Antiochian parishes in Wichita, Kansas.

SMITH, VICTORIA. Until recently an administrator in a Boston law firm, Victoria is currently involved in real estate development. She has served as Financial Advisor to the Archdiocese's Department of Religious Education and on St. Catherine's (Wollaston, MA) parish council, as well as taught Sunday School. Victoria is author of *The Bible and Our Tradition*, as well as of the *Teacher's Guide and Student Storybook* of the curriculum in religious education. She is a frequent guest speaker at various churches and schools in the Boston, New York, and Pittsburgh dioceses. She is currently pursuing Judaistic studies and Old Testament theology and leading a Bible Study group.

WALKER, BISHOP GORDON. B.A. Howard College (now Samford University), in Birmingham, Alabama, M. Div., Southwestern Baptist Theological Seminary in Fort Worth. Additional studies: Golden Gate Baptist Theological Seminary and Ohio State University. From 1952 he has served as pastor in various Baptist churches in Alabama, Texas, Ohio, and California, and has functioned in an administrative capacity for the Campus Crusade for Christ. Member and one of the original founders of the New Covenant Apostolic Order, 1973-1979. Professor of Bible at the St. Athanasius Academy of Orthodox Theology in Goleta, California, 1979 to 1982. Currently, Dean of the St. Athanasius Christian Community and Coadjutor and Diocesan Bishop of the Nashville-Atlanta Diocese of Evangelical Orthodox Church. He and his wife, former Mary Sue Henderson, have five children.

WINGENBACH, FR. GREGORY CHARLES. Received his B.A. from Goddard College in 1972 and has studied at St. Charles College, 1951-1954; University of Florida, 1955-56; St. Isaac Novitiate, 1956-57; Georgetown University, 1958-1962, and the University of Thessaloniki, 1973-1974. Received M. Div., 1976, and D. Ministry (Pastoral and Ecumenical Theology), 1982, Louisville Presbyterian Theological Seminary. A 16-year secular career included service with two major metropolitan newspapers, Federal and state government agencies, and a consortium of universities. Ordained as auxiliary deacon, 1971 and priest, 1973, he has since served parishes in America and Greece as well as in ecumenical assignments.Researched: *Richard Nixon*, 1959; *Duel at the Brink*, 1960, and *The Floating Revolution*, 1962. Wrote: *The Peace Corps*, 1961, 1963, and *Guide to the Peace Corps*, 1965. Doctoral dissertation, *The Ecumenical Movement in Orthodox Tradition*, completed in 1982, is in press at Holy Cross. He and his wife, former Mary-Ann Pearce—whose own career has encompassed "a lifetime as homemaker," plus insurance claims administration and freelance editorial proofreading for publishers—have four children, ranging from elementary school age up into the twenties.

Selected Bibliography

Mother Alexandra. *The Holy Angels*. Still River, MA: St. Bede's Publications, 1981.

The Ancient Fathers of the Desert. Translated narratives from the Evergetinos on Passions and Perfection in Christ by Archimandrite Chrysostomos. Brookline, MA: Hellenic College, Press, 1980.

Athanasius, The Life Of Anthony and the Letter To Marcellinus. Translated from the original Greek of Saint Anthanasius by Robert C. Gregg. New York: Paulist Press, 1980.

Bloom, Archbishop Anthony. *Beginning To Pray*. New York: Paulist Press, 1970.

Bloom, Archbishop Anthony. *Living Prayer*. Springfield, IL: Templegate Publishers, 1966.

Bloom, Archbishop Anthony. *Meditations: A Spiritual Journey Through the Parables*. Denville, NJ: Dimension Books, 1971.

Bulgakov, S., *The Orthodox Church*, London, 1935.

Callinicos, C. N., *The Greek Orthodox Catechism. A Manual of Instruction on Faith, Morals, and Worship*, New York: published under the Auspices of the Greek Archdiocese of North and South America, 1953.

Cavarnos, Constantine. *The Icon: Its Spiritual Basis and Purpose*. Authoritative Christian texts translated from the original Greek and edited with an introduction and notes by Constantine Cavarnos. Belmont, MA: Institute for Byzantine and Modern Greek Studies, 1973.

Orthodox Iconography. Belmont, MA: Institute for Byzantine and Modern Greek Studies, 1977.

Saint John Chrysostom. *Six Books on the Priesthood*. Translated from the Greek by Graham Neville. Crestwood, NY, St. Vladimir's Press, 1977.

Climacus, Saint John. *The Ladder of Divine Ascent*. Boston, MA: Holy Transfiguration Monastery, 1978.

A Companion to the Greek Orthodox Church. Essays and references edited by Fotios K. Litsas. New York: Department of Communication, Archdiocese of North and South America, 1984.

Coniaris, Anthony M. *Making God Real in the Orthodox Christian Home*. Minneapolis, MN: Light and Life Publishing Co., 1977.

Contemporary Issues: Orthodox Christian Perspectives by 'Exetastes'. New York: Greek Orthodox Archdiocese Press, 1976.

Saint Cyril of Jerusalem. *Lectures on the Christian Sacraments*. Edited by F. L. Gross, Crestwood, New York, St. Vladimir's Seminary Press, 1977.

Demetrakopoulos, George H., *Dictionary of Orthodox Theology, A Summary of Beliefs, Practices, and History of the Eastern Orthodox Church*, Introduction by John E. Rexine, New York: Philosophical Library, 1964.

Fedetov, G. P., ed. *A Treasury of Russian Spirituality*, Belmont, MA: Nordland, 1975.

Hackel, Sergei, *Pearl of Great Price,* "The Life of Mother Maria Skobtsova, 1891 - 1945," Crestwood, NY, St. Vladimir's Seminary Press, 1981.

Saint John of Damascus. *On the Divine Images: Three Apologies Against Those Who Attack the Divine Images.* Translated from the Greek by David Anderson. Crestwood, NY, St. Vladimir's Seminary Press, 1980.

Father John of Kronstadt. *The Spiritual Counsels of Father John of Kronstadt: Select Passages from my Life in Christ.* Edited by W. Jardine Grisbrooke. Crestwood, NY, St. Vladimir's Seminary Press, 1967.

Christ is in our Midst: Letter From a Russian Monk. Translated by Esther Williams, Crestwood, NY, St. Vladimir's Seminary Press, 1980.

Lossky, Vladimir. *Orthodox Theology: An Introduction.* Translated by Ian and Ihita Kessarcodi-Watson. Crestwood, NY, St. Vladimir's Press, 1978.

Lossky, Vladimir. *In the Image and Likeness of God.* Edited by John E. Erickson and Thomas E. Bird. Crestwood, NY, St. Vladimir's Press, 1974.

Lossky, Vladimir. *The Mystical Theology of the Eastern Church,* James Clarke & Co.: London, 1957.

Lossky, Vladimir. *The Orthodox,* Minneapolis, MN: Light and Life Publishing Co., n.d.

Meyendorff, John. *Living Tradition: Orthodox Witness in the Contemporary World.* Crestwood, NY, St. Vladimir's Seminary Press, 1978.

St. Nicodemus of the Holy Mountain and St. Makarios of Corinth, compilers. *The Philokalia,* translated and edited by G.E.H. Palmer, Philip Sherrard, and Kallistos Ware. London: Faber and Faber, 1979.

Ouspensky, Leonid. *Theology of the Icon.* Translated by Elizabeth Meyendorff. Crestwood, NY, St. Vladimir's Seminary Press, 1978.

Patrinacos, Rev. Dr. Nicon D., *The Orthodox Liturgy*, "The Greek Text of the Ecumenical Patriarchate, with a Translation into English, Together with a Study of the Development of the Orthodox Liturgy from the 2nd Century to this Day", Garwood, NJ: The Graphic Arts Press, 1976.

Philippou, A. J., ed. *The Orthodox Ethos, Studies in Orthodoxy*, "Essays in Honour of the Centenary of the Greek Orthodox Archdiocese of North and South America." Oxford, England: Holywell Press, 1954.

Poulos, George, *Orthodox Saints: Spiritual Profiles for Modern Man*. Volumes I, II, III, and IV. Brookline, MA. Holy Cross Press, 1976, 1978, 1980, 1982 respectively.

Schmemann, Alexander. *For the Life of the World: Sacraments and Orthodoxy*. Crestwood, NY, St. Vladimir's Seminary Press, 1973.

Schmemann, Alexander. *Great Lent*. Crestwood, NY, St. Vladimir's Seminary Press, 1974.

Schmemann, Alexander. *Liturgy and Life: Lectures and Essays on Christian Development through Liturgical Experience*. New York: Department of Religious Education, Orthodox Church in America, 1974.

Schmemann, Alexander. *Of Water and the Spirit: A Liturgical Study of Baptism*. Crestwood, NY, St. Vladimir's Seminary Press, 1974.

Sherrard, Philip, *The Greek East and Latin West*, London, 1959.

Sophrony, Archimandrite. *The Monk of Mount Athos: Staretz Silouan, 1866-1938*. Translated from the Russian by Rosemary Edmonds. London, Mowbrays, 1973.

Vaporis, Nomikos Michael (Ed.). *Three Byzantine Sacred Poets: Studies of Saint Romanos Melodos, Saint John of Damascus, Saint Symeon the New Theologian.* Brookline, MA: Holy Cross Orthodox Press, 1979.

Waddell, Helen, *The Desert Fathers*, London, 1936.

Ware, Timothy. *The Orthodox Church.* New York. Penguin Books, 1963.

Ware, Timothy. *The Orthodox Way.* Crestwood, NY, St. Vladimir's Seminary Press, 1979.

Ware, Timothy. *Communion and Intercommunion*, Minneapolis, MN: Light and Life Publishing Co., 1980.

Ware, Timothy. *The Power of the Name, The Jesus Prayer in Orthodox Spirituality*, SLG Press, Convent of the Incarnation, Fairacres, Oxford, Publication #43, 1981.

The Way of a Pilgrim and *The Pilgrim Continues His Way*. Translated from the Russian by R. M. French. New York: The Seabury Press, 1965.

Weil, Simone, *Intimations of Christianity Among the Ancient Greeks*, collected and translated from the French by Elizabeth Chase Geissbuhler, Boston, Beacon Press, 1958.